What Other
Marital Intelligence

As I read this book, I thought—"It's about time!" A gifted author, communicator, and leader, Dr. Gil Stieglitz has just delivered his most valuable book. *Marital Intelligence* is a gold mine for anyone who believes that any marriage can thrive if and when biblical hope and help are applied. And this is no mere ivory tower treatise. Drawing from 25 years of experience, Gil uncovers the five basic problems in marriage and then offers the two things all marriages need—encouragement and practical help straight from the Scriptures. This book will help couples who are struggling and those who want to add a new spark to their marriage. It will also be a great resource for counselors, pastors, and premarital workshops. This is a must-read that will energize and equip marriages!

What's at stake? Everything! Because I believe that what happens in your house is as important as what happens in the White House, my prayer is that God will use this book to light some fires in thousands of homes that will never go out.

Ray Johnston, *Pastor, Bayside Church, Granite Bay, California*

Finally, a book that does more than just tell you that you are not doing marriage the right way, but gives you day by day practical ways to make it right! It's the kind of map you can use in your marriage—and give to others to help their marriage.

Dean Matteson, *Senior Pastor, Faith Community Church, Palmdale, California.*

Gil Stieglitz is the most strategic writer in the current church world. His understanding and experience as a pastor, district superintendent, consultant and husband have combined to produce a rich background captured for this book. He has brought the best of current marriage theory, counseling background, and biblical principles to bear on a fresh, comprehensive look at our most intimate relationship—marriage. Whether you are contemplating marriage, are newly married or are committed to a long-term marriage, you will find accurate diagnosis, self-evaluation, and practical help. If applied, this book can help save a deteriorating marriage, restore a drifting marriage, and add depth to a good marriage. Whatever condition you bring to the book, get ready for a great read and then practical suggestions to improve on your relationship.

Dr. Conrad Lowe, *Senior Pastor, Exec. Pastor, District Supervisor, and Consultant*

At last! A marriage resource manual and enrichment guide for the rest of us who want biblical, honest answers but don't want psycho-jargon! The self-test alone is easy to use, helpful, and worth the price of the book. Together with the book's practical advice, this test and book will give real feedback and guidance to hurting couples who know their marriage is broken but don't know how to fix it. Many couples will have Gil Stieglitz to thank for improving their marriage! Way to go, Gil!

Dr. Rick Stedman, *Senior Pastor, Adventure Christian Church, Author of* Your Single Treasure: Good News About Singles and Sexuality.

If you have ever been frustrated that marriage didn't come with a manual, you just hit the jackpot! *Marital Intelligence* by Gil Stieglitz will provide you with a roadmap for increasing the health, stability, and foundations of your marriage. Gil's book is organized around the five problems in marriage; but rather than being a book about how to avoid or resolve conflicts alone, this book equips you to build a healthy marriage in each of the five problem areas. I strongly recommend the book for pastors, counselors, and anyone wanting to build or bless others with a strong marriage.

Dr. John Jackson, *Executive Director of Thriving Churches International, Author of* Leveraging Your Communication Style *and* Leveraging Your Leadership Style

Marital
Intelligence

Marital Intelligence

Gil Stieglitz

BMH Books
www.bmhbooks.com
Winona Lake, IN 46590

Marital Intelligence
A Foolproof Guide for Saving and Supercharging Marriages

Copyright © Gil Stieglitz 2010

ISBN: 978-0-88469-265-2
RELIGION / Christian Ministry / Counseling & Recovery

Published by BMH books, Winona Lake, IN 46590
www.bmhbooks.com

Dedication

This book is dedicated to my incredible wife, Dana.

Being married to you is a sheer joy. Our marriage has been a journey of constant and regular delight. People don't believe me when I share what it is like to have you as my wife. In this relationship called marriage you make me appear more intelligent than I am. I find myself constantly attracted to you—spirit, soul, and body. I could not have asked for a better life partner. It is the wonder of being married to you that gives me energy, beauty, and inspiration. You truly are God's gift to me.

Table of Contents

Problem #3: Clashing Temperaments

Problem #4: Competing Relationships

Problem #5: Past Baggage

Acknowledgments

No book could be produced without the many people behind the scenes that make it happen. First, I thank my incredible wife, Dana, and my lovely daughters, Jenessa, Abbey, and Grace, who have allowed me to spend endless hours working on this book. They share my goal to help other families obtain what we have.

I also thank Sandy Johnson, my administrative assistant at Principles to Live By, and Dalene Lequieu, my administrative assistant with the Western District of the Evangelical Free Churches of America. They have allowed me to remain sane while working with those non-profit organizations.

Thank you Gary and Susan Basham, Jud and Mary Boies, Kyle and Meredith Hedwall, Ken Townsend and Dave Doty for providing valuable suggestions on the raw manuscript. Many thanks to Vickie Newman, who worked so hard to edit the original manuscript. To the folks at BMH Books, thank you for working alongside me to print this important resource.

Last, but not least, I thank the willing couples I have worked with in their moments of need for the last 30 years. The wonder of seeing a marriage saved is amazing. The power of supercharging a marriage formerly in business mode is thrilling. Thank you for allowing me to apply God's principles to your marriage.

Gil Stieglitz
Roseville, California
September 2009

How to Use this Book

This book was written so that Christians, counselors, and leaders would have a biblical and practical guide to help marriages. Each concept includes an exercise to apply that biblical truth in one's life and marriage. Therefore if the exercises are not attempted, the book will be of little value. The genius of the book (if there is any) is not what I write but what the reader will do through the exercises at the end of each section.

Personal Study

This book can be a personal study. If you are working through this book alone, take the test in each chapter, pick one truth in that chapter, and do one of the exercises that accompany that idea. Some exercises need to be practiced for a week before their effectiveness can be evaluated. If you find an exercise that is not helpful, simply move on to the next one. Do not be in a hurry to get through the book. Let the power of the biblical exercises go through you. If you find that one exercise is particularly helpful, stay with it for a month or longer. In fact, that effective exercise may become the impetus for changing your marriage. It is more important that you discover how to make a difference in your marriage than that you finish the book in a certain time. It may take a year or longer to go through the entire book. After you have finished it as a personal study, you may want to join a group study in which you will go through the material with your spouse or others.

Mentor-Directed Study

This book can be studied in a mentor-directed format, where a well-respected, godly leader takes an individual or small group through the material and evaluates the progress. Each week or month the mentor assigns specific chapters and exercises for study and action.

At the next meeting significant time will be given to describing what happened when you did the exercises. If they were not done or were not done well, the same exercises should be repeated. It is crucial not to be in hurry to get through the material. It is far more important that the biblical material bring about lasting change and impact. In my opinion the mentor-directed study is one of the most powerful and effective ways of teaching biblical material. A mentor-directed study is even more effective when the person with the desire for a mentor asks someone he or she highly respects to mentor him or her in studying this material.

A second way to initiate a mentor-directed study is for the mentor to ask the Lord to direct him to those who are ready for a deeper spiritual growth study like this one. He then asks the people whom God has put on his heart if they would be interested in growing through a weekly study of this type. If they say yes, he can put them in a small group of people like themselves.

Class or Lecture series

This book can be covered as a Bible study class or adult Sunday School class. If there are fewer than six people in the class, I recommend that you adopt the mentor format rather than the class style. But if there are seven or more, the lecture style can work quite well. This study or one like it should be a constantly repeating component of leadership development in every church. If you would like to use the prepared presentation slides that go along with this book, you can download the PowerPoint slides from the Principles to Live By website (www.ptlb.com). Please feel free to use those slides in the class.

The best class format divides an hour and a half into three segments of approximately 30 minutes. Start with prayer and about 20-30 minutes of sharing in small groups of 3-4 people about how the exercises went from the previous week. (This material is of such a nature that same-gender groups usually work best.) If there is widespread misunderstanding on the exercises that were taught previously, they should be explained again and assigned again.

Next, there should be a 20-30 minute lecture on the next material. The teacher should determine how much material is covered each meeting. Sometimes the information and/or exercises are so crucial that a very limited amount of material should be the complete focus for that session. The goal is not to have people impressed with the teacher, but to build, save, and strengthen marriages. That will happen only if the participants are actually doing the exercises.

Finally, 20-30 minutes should be set aside for actually working on the exercises in class. Have the students try out the ideas and exercises by themselves or with their spouse. Then have each person in the class commit to doing particular exercises during the next week. Remember, if a project or exercise needs to be repeated, repeat it. The focus is on doing the work not covering the material. At the end of each of the chapters of this book there are exercises. Do at least one of those exercises after each study.

Because the church is always in need of strong marriages, I strongly suggest that in every church the material in this book or material like it should be scheduled continually or a marriage support group established.

Marital Intelligence

Introduction

Introduction

There are only five problems in marriage. Every time I make that statement, people think I'm crazy or starting a joke! But I am completely serious. After conducting thousands of hours of counseling and witnessing the saving of hundreds of marriages on the brink of disaster, I confidently assert there are only five problems in marriage. They are:

1. Ignoring needs
2. Immature behaviors
3. Clashing temperaments
4. Competing relationships
5. Past baggage.

Marital Intelligence understands these five problems and their solutions. The more you understand these problems and practice their solutions, the higher your Marital IQ. Every marriage will encounter difficulty as two people try to make their relationship successful. Pinpoint those issues and apply their solutions, and you'll do just that.

Most people today are living relationally unconscious. No one seems to know how to make marriages work. Unfortunately, the problem is not helped by much of today's marital counseling. One of the dirty little secrets of marriage counseling, both religious and secular, is that it largely fails. Statistics confirm that 75% of those who seek marriage counseling get a divorce anyway. A high percentage of those who sought counseling to help their marriage believe that it actually harmed their marriage.[1]

A number of years ago, various individuals independently began offering a different kind of marriage counseling.[2] The focus of this kind of counseling is on restoring love, happiness, and joy to the relationship through positive actions. This focus has proven to restore marriages and cause them to thrive. To be intelligent about marriage, we must identify the key problems and implement practical solutions that will inject new levels of happiness, love, and joy.

If you were to come to me for marriage counseling, I would show you the chart below and explain each of the five problems. I would then ask you to rank the problems in terms of their level of disruption in your marriage. In other words, answer the question, "Which is the greatest problem in your marriage, the second greatest, the third, and so on?"

Ignoring Needs	Immature Behaviors	Clashing Temperaments	Competing Relationships	Past Baggage

A marriage almost always breaks down along these lines. If a couple applies the appropriate solutions to the particular problem, the relationship improves and usually begins to thrive. Each of the sections in this book deals with one of these major problems in marriage.

When I describe these five problems, what once seemed hopeless and irreconcilable is quantified and the troubled couple can see solutions for the first time. These solutions require work, but knowing a marriage is salvageable gives hope. The chart focuses our discussion on the couple's specific areas of need. That is immensely superior to having a couple fight about trivial things in front of the counselor, making no progress on the real issues in the marriage.

If your marriage is in trouble, this book is the right resource for you. Each section and each chapter is full of practical changes that will make a significant difference in your marriage. If you need a quick cheat sheet for your marriage, the Marriage Intelligence Test statements (in each section of this book or the full version in Appendix 1), describe the minimum requirements of a great marriage. Remember, it will take time to improve your marriage. Now is a great time to get started.

If you want to help people with damaged or broken marriages this book is just what you need. It allows the marriage counselor to quickly and powerfully identify and provide solutions to the real problems in a marriage. This "schematic" on marriage gives hope and allows the counselor to offer real world solutions that will immediately improve the relationship.[3]

Problem #1

Ignoring Needs

Problem #1

Ignoring Needs

Overview

Daniel called me in a panic. His wife, Marlene, demanded he quit his job or she would leave. Everything he ever wanted was dying: his career, his marriage, and his family. How did this happen? What could he do? Was there any way to save his marriage? His career? Was there a way to save his life? I listened to his explanation for about an hour, and then I suggested his problem was that his wife didn't feel honored. That sounded too simplistic to Daniel. Surely Marlene would not destroy their lives, his career, and their children over a lack of honor!

I explained honor wasn't merely something Marlene wanted; it was a fundamental need. Without honor, a woman withers and no longer sees the point of the marriage; it becomes a useless charade. Every day she waits for her husband to value her ideas and contributions. Every day she longs for his attention. But in many cases, it never comes. Days without honor are like a starvation diet, and eventually a woman can't take the deprivation anymore. She doesn't receive enough from the marriage to tolerate the hassles of married life, so she leaves. Perhaps she'll leave physically or emotionally, psychologically, or even morally. Her soul receives nothing from her husband, so what's the point? It isn't that he forgot her birthday. It's that every day she is slammed with the reality that she doesn't matter to him. His job is more important, his television programs are more important, the kids are more important, his hobbies are more important, and the latest phone call is more important—almost everything takes precedence over her. The devalued wife realizes she is very low on his list of priorities. It is the accumulation of these blows that requires she take action. She needs and expects so much from this man but feels more like an employee than a wife.

I explained to Daniel that even though he doesn't have a huge need for honor from his wife, she really needs it from him. He needs different things from her. He doesn't wonder whether she is thinking about him. He doesn't need to know where he is on her priority list, but she needs to know where she is on his. If Daniel focused on lifting Marlene's value to his first priority for three months, he could win her back (assuming there wasn't another man). He told me she didn't even want to see or talk with him. I suggested several ways to demonstrate she is the most important person in his life.

He had his doubts, but he tried my recommendations. He began to honor her. He resigned from the job that kept him away so many hours. He realized he could get another job but didn't want another wife. He took a job that allowed him maximum time to be with her and the kids. He learned how to value her and put her first in his life every day. He gave her and the children significant amounts of attention and involvement. Within three months, she was drawn back into the marriage. When I spoke with her, she explained her marriage was better than ever. Over the next two years, Daniel continually showed Marlene that she was the most valuable person in his life. She began to blossom and grow, even making her own needed changes.

The first component of Marital Intelligence is recognizing that men and women have different relational needs, and they cannot be ignored. Marriage is where our deepest relational needs are to be met.[1] The more they are met, the more joy and happiness we experience. The more our relational needs are ignored, the less joy and happiness we experience. Because men and women approach marriage looking for different relational needs, marriage can be a disaster without some direction. But if both husband and wife are willing to learn how to meet their spouse's relational needs, marriage can become a source of endless delight and refreshment. This section is an overview of how to become loving husbands and wives by meeting those different relational needs. For fuller treatment of these essential relational needs, see my two previous books: *Becoming a Godly Husband* and *Becoming a Godly Wife*.[2]

The Definition of Love

To understand how to make a marriage work, you must have a working definition of love. To love means to meet needs, to pursue, and to please. Marriage works when both husband and wife commit themselves to increasing those kinds of actions flowing between them. In doing so we are following God's example of love. God demonstrated His love when He chose to meet the desperate need of the human condition (Rom. 5:8). He chose to pursue us when we were unable and uninterested in pursuing Him (Luke 15). He chose to please us with wonderful gifts we didn't deserve that go beyond the forgiveness in salvation (Rom. 5:1; James 1:17). In connection with marriage, as I choose to meet my spouse's relational needs, I am loving her. When I pursue my wife's soul (thinking, emotions, personality, morality, and spirituality), I love her no matter what emotions arise within me. When I act to please my spouse (emotionally, physically, spiritually, mentally, or recreationally), I love her whether or not I feel romantic. There has been an overemphasis in our generation on whether one *feels* like loving the other person. Love does not begin with a feeling; it begins with a choice. This choice is then followed by actions to meet needs, to pursue, or to please. Emotions and feelings are reactions to the choices and actions of others.

Great marriages develop because at least one person acts to meet the needs of his or her partner, acts to pursue the partner's soul, and acts to please him or her. This sets off a wonderful chain reaction of positive emotions and feelings in and for each other. But it began with the right action, not the feeling. To improve our marriages, we must increase actions that meet needs and pursue and/or please each other. When both parties are seeking to act in these positive ways, a great marriage is produced. If the husband or wife ignores these needs, pursues personal interests, and/or focuses on his or her own pleasure, the marriage will be miserable for both of them.

Marriage starts out easy, but it usually becomes difficult. During dating and courtship there is a natural ability to meet the needs of the other person. The magic of infatuation draws out the ability to meet relational needs, pursue the inner person, and the desire to please them. But at some point in every marriage, it becomes work to meet those same needs. It is at this point that men and women must choose to meet their partners' needs regardless of what they feel. If a husband or wife backs off on meeting his or her spouse's relational needs, the marriage will experience diminished joy almost immediately. If this continues, the same couple that was madly in love will begin to entertain thoughts of separation and even divorce. It is devastating to be in a marriage where our needs are ignored or disregarded. To have the marriage you desire, you must meet each other's deepest relational needs.

The Golden Rule

One of the secrets to a great marriage is the Golden Rule. Matthew 7:12 says, "Do to others what you would have them do to you" (NIV). If you would like your partner to meet your needs, then meet your partner's first. Stop hoping your spouse will be the initiator of love. Draw him or her in by active love. Whatever you want him/her to do for you, do it first. Begin meeting your spouse's greatest relational need, and after time passes, ask him or her to do the same.

This is the quickest way to dramatic marital improvement. Dedicate yourself to meeting the relational needs of your spouse and discuss with your spouse how to best meet your own needs. God has detailed in the Scriptures how to become the husband or wife that meets your spouse's needs. He instructs the husband to do specific things to minister to his wife. He instructs the wife to do certain things to meet the needs of her husband. God knows men and women have different needs, so He gives different commands for both in their marital roles.[3]

The Needs of Wives	The Needs of Husbands
Honor	Respect
Understanding	Adaptation
Security	Domestic Leadership
Building Unity	Intimacy
Agreement	Companionship
Nurture *Leadership, communication, romance, tender touch*	Attractive Soul and Body
Defender	Listening

For a man to be a truly loving husband, he must honor his wife (1 Peter 3:7), understand his wife (1 Peter 3:7), make her feel secure (Eph. 5:29), build strong bonds of unity between them (Gen. 2:24; Prov. 15:31-32), seek oneness through a system of agreement (Eph. 5:23, Amos 3:3), nurture her with communication, romance, tender touch, and wise leadership (Eph. 5:29), and defend her from any and all threats (Eph. 5:29). If a man does these things, he will be a great husband. Each woman is unique, and a great husband will find the best ways to encourage and love his wife throughout his lifetime. But the basic elements of love are these bottom line relational needs: honor, understanding, security, building unity, agreement, nurture (leadership, communication, romance, tender touch), and defense. The successful husband focuses on them daily.

For a woman to be a truly loving wife, she needs to respect her husband (Eph. 5:33), adapt to him (Eph. 5:22), use her leadership skills in the home (1 Tim. 5:14; Titus 2:5), embrace her husband's recurring need for physical intimacy (1 Cor. 7:3-5), become his companion (Titus 2:4), build an increasingly attractive soul while maintaining an attractive body (1 Peter 3:1-4), and listen to the depths of his soul without reaction (1 Peter 3:4; Titus 2:5). God commissions a wife to enable her husband to succeed (Gen. 2:20). Each man needs a loving wife who builds him up, allowing him to reach his maximum potential. Every man is unique, and his wife will spend a lifetime learning how to assist him for maximum effectiveness. The principles that frame her efforts are respect, adaptation, domestic leadership, intimacy, companionship, attractive soul and body, and listening.

When a man and woman step into their roles and dedicate themselves to meeting each other's relational needs, the marriage is headed for greatness. There will be times when someone unfairly gives more than the other, but with understanding and clear communication, it will balance out. On the other hand, if either partner ignores the other's needs, the marriage is rapidly headed for a fall.

If we see our spouse's needs like a job description, we must act to meet needs or the "partnership" will fail. Begin accomplishing things that will thrill your spouse and transform your marriage into a wonderful partnership.

Marriage is a covenant before God in which two people meet their spouse's needs, pursue them, and please them. Are you meeting your spouse's needs and pursuing and pleasing him or her? Would your spouse give you a positive yearly review? Or does your spouse want to fire you for failure to carry out what you promised?

Marriage Solutions and Exercises

- Dedicate one hour every day to meet the needs of your spouse.

- Make thoughtful, calm requests for your spouse to meet your relational needs.

- What caused you to fall in love in the first place? Start doing those things again.

- Explore your spouse's soul through questions about his or her dreams, past, friends, interests, fantasies, feelings, odd thoughts, opinions, spirituality, enemies, new ideas, joys, potential interests, dislikes, fears, and temptations.

- Inquire and experiment with what might please your spouse.

- Ask your spouse to do something that would really please you.

Marital Intelligence Test

This test probes the actions necessary to have a great marriage. Do not be surprised by the results. Celebrate your strengths and work on improving your weak areas. Your spouse might respond differently to the same questions. These areas of differences are opportunities to grow and improve your marriage. Hopefully this test will whet your appetite for the solutions in this book.

Marital Intelligence Test
Respond to the following statements using the following scale: 0 = Never; 1 = Rarely; 2 = Occasionally; 3 = Sometimes; 4 = Usually; 5 = Always

Problem #1	
I compliment my spouse every day.	0 1 2 3 4 5
I understand and accept how my spouse thinks.	0 1 2 3 4 5
I am involved in our home and family to the satisfaction of my spouse.	0 1 2 3 4 5
My spouse feels secure financially, emotionally, physically, and morally.	0 1 2 3 4 5
I touch my spouse tenderly and hug him/her often.	0 1 2 3 4 5
I talk and listen to my spouse about an hour each day.	0 1 2 3 4 5
My spouse and I go on a date once a week.	0 1 2 3 4 5
I give my spouse at least one hour of focused attention each day.	0 1 2 3 4 5
I admire my spouse and he/she knows it.	0 1 2 3 4 5
I have adapted to my spouse's likes, dislikes, career, style, schedule, etc.	0 1 2 3 4 5
I work hard to make sure our home and family are the best they can be.	0 1 2 3 4 5
I meet my spouse's sexual needs.	0 1 2 3 4 5

I do things with my spouse that he/she enjoys.	0 1 2 3 4 5
I work hard at being grateful, kind, sympathetic, healthy, and attractive to my spouse.	0 1 2 3 4 5
I pursue the soul of my spouse by listening to what he/she says and doesn't say.	0 1 2 3 4 5
My spouse and I come to agreement before we make major decisions.	0 1 2 3 4 5
I receive a compliment daily from my spouse.	0 1 2 3 4 5
I believe my spouse understands the real me and does not demand that I change.	0 1 2 3 4 5
I feel that my spouse is fully engaged in the life of our family.	0 1 2 3 4 5
I am confident that my spouse would never damage our relationship financially, emotionally, verbally, physically, sexually, or morally.	0 1 2 3 4 5
I receive enough hugs and nonsexual touches from my spouse to meet my emotional needs.	0 1 2 3 4 5
My spouse actively listens to me daily.	0 1 2 3 4 5
I feel that my spouse wants to be with me romantically, mentally, and physically.	0 1 2 3 4 5
I feel admired and respected by my spouse.	0 1 2 3 4 5
My likes, dislikes, ideas, and desires are reflected in our relationship.	0 1 2 3 4 5
I enjoy spending time at home with my family.	0 1 2 3 4 5
My spouse understands and meets my sexual needs.	0 1 2 3 4 5
My spouse enjoys doing things together that are important to me.	0 1 2 3 4 5
I am more attracted to my spouse each year because he/she is kinder, more grateful, more encouraging, and takes care of him/herself.	0 1 2 3 4 5

I feel my spouse cares deeply for the real me.	0 1 2 3 4 5
Subtotal Section #1	

Add up your total. How did you do? These results reflect the current condition of your relationship. Realize no one is the perfect spouse. You know you haven't been perfect, and you shouldn't expect your husband or wife to be either. You both have weak areas, but with time and effort, your marriage can improve. The solutions in this book *will* work.

The positive statements on the test detail a high standard of how to treat each other. Start applying those truths, and your relationship will improve right away.

Scoring

150 - 113: You have a very good marriage in this area. Keep it up. Have a discussion with your spouse about how to meet each other's needs even more effectively, how to pursue each other's soul, and how to please him or her even more.

112 - 76: You have a good marriage that could be significantly improved by meeting more relational needs. Pick one or two needs you will start to meet at a new level. Ask which needs are most important to your spouse. Calmly ask your spouse to meet one of your needs at a new level.

75 - 38: There are some serious deficiencies in love in your marriage. Both of you feel your relational needs are not being met. Your marriage is moving into a business-type relationship. Begin doing one new thing each day to meet each other's relational needs. Participating in a small group with other couples might help to focus the changes.

37 - 0: Love is lacking in your marriage. The answer to the pain and loneliness is to start meeting each other's relational needs. It takes only one person in the marriage to make a difference in the beginning. Schedule a meeting with a counselor or pastor.

Becoming a Loving Husband

In this section I will give an overview of the husband's role in loving his wife. This will be an intense learning process, but it will yield rich rewards. Marriages make dramatic improvement when the husband begins to fulfill his role.

Honor

I feel ignored, unimportant, and devalued.

Bill showed me the note on the refrigerator that his wife Angie had left. "I can't take it anymore," it read. She was gone. And so were the kids. Bill called me in a panic to try to understand what happened. Up to the moment he found the note, he would have said he had a good, if not great, marriage. What he didn't realize was that he was starving his wife of the value she craved. She needed him to honor her, and he clearly wasn't. She was the last thing on his mind, and she knew it. His job, his children, his TV, his tools, his hobbies, and his friends were more important. When devaluation reached its lowest point, she grabbed the kids and left.

It took two weeks to get Bill to really understand that she left because of something he wasn't doing. I explained to him that, according to the Bible, a wife needs to be honored as the most important person, place, or thing in her husband's life or she won't be able to respond to him (Eph. 5:25; 1 Peter 3:7). When his wife confirmed she felt devalued by the time and attention he lavished on everyone and everything but her, it finally clicked. He was a changed man. He began to honor her every day and quickly saved his marriage.

The Bible says in 1 Peter 3:7, "You husbands…grant her honor as a fellow heir of the grace of life, so that your prayers will not be hindered." Thus the Bible declares men must honor their wives. The word *honor* means "to be weighty, valuable." When used as a verb, it means "to add value, to treat someone as highly valuable" and "to increase this value by honorable behavior." A wife needs her husband to add value to her. When it is clear her husband places her in the primary position in his life, she is energized by his love to be all she can be and to respond enthusiastically. But when other things are more important, it is difficult for her to respond to him.

A wife wants to know what level of importance she has in her husband's priority structure. Often she will run tests to determine her level of importance. She may ask questions like, "Did you think about me today?" She may want to talk when all he wants to do is get in the recliner. She may ask him to take out the trash to see if her needs are more important than his desires. These tests are not silly. They are a way of determining her level of importance. If her husband highly values her, her need for honor is met, and she can easily engage in the marriage relationship. If her husband is too busy with his own interests, she concludes she isn't valuable.

Marriage Solutions and Exercises

- Compliment your wife every day. Do this verbally, in writing, or tangibly.

- Expect your wife to test whether she is number one in your world every day.

- Call her during the day and tell her you love her.

- During the day write down questions to ask her, stories you want to share, and ideas you want to discuss.

Understanding
I feel misunderstood, run over, blamed, and uncared for.

Jim was never wrong. At least in *his* mind. His unwillingness to admit his mistakes, shortcomings, and weaknesses had a devastating impact on his wife Esther. She learned to power up and be angry and insensitive for pure survival. When Esther left, Jim was forced to admit he didn't understand his wife or how to build a mutually satisfying marriage. It took three weeks of intensive education before Jim was willing to learn how to treat her differently. After his change of heart, Esther was willing to come back.

He had to admit when he was wrong. He had to realize his wife was different in many ways. He had to learn her preferences, her temperament, her abilities, and her dreams. Jim had to accept the responsibility of becoming a truly loving husband. It represented a total transformation. Jim changed and saved his marriage.

The Scriptures are clear about the husband's responsibility to build a marriage for two people, not just for himself. "You husbands likewise, live with your wives in an understanding way, as with a weaker vessel, since she is a woman" (1 Peter 3:7). The word *weaker* means "more fragile, delicate," and even "more highly prized." The idea is not that a woman is inferior; rather she is more sensitive. Her husband must understand this difference. A man must prepare to appreciate his wife's sensitivity. That means he must be willing to quickly admit when he is wrong. He should be conscious of her unique gifts, talents, dreams, and preferences. Most successful marriages involve a man who has learned to live with his wife in an understanding way. Many dysfunctional marriages involve a man who can't see beyond his own point of view.

A husband needs to grow in four specific actions: First, he must know how to offer an effective apology. Second, he ought to know his wife's strong points and flaws, so he can emphasize her strengths and minimize her weaknesses. Third, he must understand a full picture of her temperament and how it differs from his. Fourth, he needs to know her dreams and desires, so he can help her achieve all she can for God's glory. If a husband will do those four things, his wife will overflow with love for him and become a radiant woman for God's glory.

Marriage Solutions and Exercises

- Apologize for a specific wrong and ask for forgiveness. The perceptive husband is apologizing at least once a month.

- "Honey, I was wrong when I _____. I am sorry that I acted that way. Please forgive me. Will you forgive me?"

- Make a list of your wife's 25 strengths and five weaknesses. Ask her to also make a list of her top 25 strengths. Compare the lists.

- Ask, "If everything were to happen perfectly in the next three years, what would you accomplish and how would your life be different?" Also ask, "What stands in the way of accomplishing those dreams and goals?" Listen. Do not become negative or explain why her dreams won't happen. Your purpose is to listen to her heart.

Security

I am afraid of your anger, your financial decisions, your words, our physical environment, and/or your negative comparisons of me with other women.

Joe didn't have a clue that he was destroying his marriage. In his mind, it was Beth's fault. She constantly nagged at him. She didn't trust him. *She* was the problem. What Joe didn't understand was that his actions and reactions were severely damaging his wife's security in the marriage. It was this insecurity that caused her to ask questions, probe about his whereabouts, and look into his spending. In the past, Joe plunged the couple into debt through impulsive purchases. They struggled under the weight of creditors and bills. The couple didn't have much money, so Beth was naturally concerned when non-budgeted items were purchased. Was he back to his old tricks? Where did we get the money for this? Why did he think we needed this? To complicate matters, Joe had a temper and occasionally blew up in rage. He broke things when he was angry. Whenever she found something broken, she naturally wondered if Joe had flown into a rage and broken it.

It didn't matter if Joe felt his anger issues and impulsive spending were in the past. Beth needed constant demonstration that his old practices were not resurfacing. She needed to feel secure in their relationship.

The Scriptures are clear that a husband must meet this need in his wife. "Husbands, love your wives, just as Christ also loved the church and gave Himself up for her ... So husbands ought also to love their own wives as their own bodies. He who loves his own wife loves himself; for no one ever hated his own flesh, but nourishes and cherishes it, just as Christ also does the church" (Eph. 5:25, 28-29). Notice that God tells husbands to cherish their wives. To cherish means to protect and defend. Men can quickly destroy marital joy by foolish financial dealings, unsafe physical conditions, emotionally abusive words and situations, and comparisons to other women. Most men stand ready to protect and defend their wives from physical threats but miss defending her from emotional, mental, spiritual, financial, and relational threats. It is the non-physical areas of security that baffle men like Joe. When a man grasps all the ways he is to provide security, he becomes the husband his wife needs him to be. He is to meet this need for security in four ways: financially, emotionally, romantically, and relationally.

A husband is to provide financial security by his income, resourcefulness, hard work, and skillful management of the finances. If a man refuses to provide for his family financially, a woman's security can be shattered. It is his responsibility to make sure there is money for essentials. This creates security, even if he is gone more than she wants or must say no to something she wants to have. I remember working with one man who refused to work and yet still wanted a loving marriage and family. He destroyed his marriage by his refusal to provide financial stability.

A husband is to provide emotional security by the way he speaks and acts around his wife. If he can't control his anger or if he uses words that hurt, he will damage his wife's ability to respond to him. A woman cannot be expected to respond positively under the threat of emotional outbursts, physical violence, or verbal assaults. Unfortunately many men don't understand how sensitive a woman is to the emotional climate of the home, and they resent their wives' sensitivity. God gives this sensitivity to the woman so she can help her man grow and reach his fullest potential both at home and in his career. A wife's sensitivity is a gift of God to her husband.

A husband is to provide romantic security by acting and speaking positively into his wife's life. If a man compares his wife to other women or constantly stares at them, it creates a negative sense of security in her. Our current culture dumps huge insecurity issues on women, especially about body image. It is too much to bear for most women to have insecurities, comparisons, and imperfections pointed out by their husbands. A husband needs to build his wife up with words of encouragement if he expects her to respond to him.

A husband is also to provide physical security. That doesn't mean that *he* feels safe; it means that *she* feels safe in the environment around her. Do her home and neighborhood feel safe to her? How can he make his wife feel more secure physically? If a husband leaves his wife in an unsafe environment for a long time, it will deeply impact her because she feels unprotected. It is important that he does not judge the security of his family solely from his point of view.

Marriage Solutions and Exercises

- Does the wife feel secure in the following areas?
  o Financial: money, cash flow, and savings
  o Emotional: harmony, peace, aligned expectations, no anger, and no abuse
  o Moral: conscience, guilt, shame, and righteous behavior
  o Physical: home security, safety, no violence, and no threats
  o Verbal: no abuse, positive and affirming words, and commitment
  o Mental: honesty, no deception, no head games, and no power plays
- Discuss one positive change to improve the security in your marriage.

Building Unity

I feel like your slave, your adversary at times,
alienated from the good times, resented, and not on your team.

Most married women might ask, "How can I get my husband to be more engaged at home? It's like he's a zombie." Most men treat time at home as time off, instead of the most important part of the day. Careers require lots of time and energy these days, but the main reason for work is to provide for the family. Sometimes that idea is lost when the emotional rewards at work are more alluring than those at home. But the greatest long-term rewards in life come from a great marriage and an enjoyable family. Men naturally feel the temptation to make a name for themselves in the world, but the most important names we create are "great husband" and "great father." If we can bring the level of leadership we use at work to our homes, our marriages would dramatically improve.

Every married man is on a high priority team called his home team. Its members desperately need him to be an active member every day because they are looking to him for leadership on the team. Most men don't grasp the essential need to lead the home through presence, involvement, and decision-making. When a wife senses her husband is maximally engaged at home, it encourages something deep within her. She knows her husband is a winner, and she is freed up to respond in love and respect for him. But if he conquers worlds, wins prestigious awards, and single-handedly saves the whales but remains disengaged at home, his leadership doesn't mean squat.

Men need to show up emotionally at home. They must engage and lead the family with their wife. That means daily and weekly planning for what the kids need to work on, how to spend money, the emotional obstacles their wife and family face, what changes are needed in the home, where to vacation, details for the couple's weekly date, etc. Our culture clearly has made a separation between family and work, but husbands must bring their leadership and abilities to the home.

Another way a husband builds unity is to ensure his wife is never the enemy. It may be the boss, the company, a relative, or the government, but your wife is never the enemy. The husband must draw the line, so he and his wife are always on the same side. The only exception is if the husband or wife is perpetually violating the law of God.

The husband must also stay engaged to build good memories. A wife and family live in the memories of the good times. He needs to make sure vacations and get-a-ways are planned. He needs to make sure his family experiences fun times together. That includes dates with the kids, family outings, and special times one on one with each of the kids.

Marriage Solutions and Exercises

- Ask your wife in what ways she needs you to be involved at home.

- Plan a vacation or get-a-way within the next three months.
- Schedule a "staff meeting" with your wife. Cover the following topics:
  o Schedules, children, work, finances, church, dreams
  o Marriage positives and potential marriage improvements

Agreement
I am afraid of impulsive, unwise, or unilateral decisions.

Rhonda and James couldn't agree on anything except that their marriage was not working. They argued about everything. If James said something, Rhonda contested. If Rhonda tried to tell her story, James interrupted. Whenever they tried to buy something or decide what to do with the children, it was a disaster. I realized these two had never worked through a decision in which both agreed. I taught them a simple five-step process for making decisions. A counselor friend starts his marriage counseling with this system because it is helpful for couples to relax. The system comes from an application of Amos 3:3: "Can two walk together except they be agreed?" (KJV). These steps include a discussion phase, an options phase, a counsel phase, a prayer phase, and a decision phase.

The first step is the discussion phase. Someone proposes an idea, and the idea is explored. Questions are asked and reasons are probed. No decision can be made during this phase. It is important for both to share their ideas without being shut down, judged, or belittled. Discussion does not equal decision. In many homes, people never get to explore their ideas with their spouse because there is an implied action. It can be very beneficial if both people feel their ideas will get a hearing with honest interaction and consideration. That builds trust and openness. Most ideas never make it past the discussion phase, but it is important to take time to discuss it.

If there is still a desire to pursue the idea after the discussion phase, it is time for the options phase, when the idea is explored through possible ways of accomplishing it.

Here's a real example to make it more concrete. Let's say your wife thinks the family needs a new car. The first step in making the decision is to discuss her interest. You ask the questions: who, what, when, where, why, and how. If after discussion, you both feel it makes sense to move forward, you then begin an options discussion. It might begin like this: "If we were to get a new car, let's ask these questions even if we have different ideas at this point."

"What kind of car do you think we need? Name the top five in order of preference."

"How much should we spend?"

"How should we pay for the car?"

"When do we need it?"

Other questions may arise that will allow you to think through several tentative plans. Remember that nothing has been decided—it is still a discussion of options that may or may not happen. The options phase may last for weeks or months as you talk about various possibilities.

The third phase is the counsel phase. Both parties suggest whom you would like to consult for information or advice. It is often helpful to ask each other, "Whom should I talk to to make a wise decision?" Create a list and consult the resources. When my wife and I reach this point, she always suggests we talk with her father. I always suggest we talk with *my* father. Other resources may include Consumer Reports, Internet reviews, experts, friends, coworkers, relatives, and so on. Everyone finds it helpful to check with people who know more before decision-making. Spouses who just want to do what they want often skip this step because they don't want disagreement with their plan. If you want to make wise decisions, don't skip this step. It may take weeks or months to check these resources, but good decisions usually take time.

The fourth phase is to pray together. Ask God to guide you to the right people, resources, and information so you can make a wise decision. Ask God to make both of you sensitive to wisdom and not just your own way. Some people think prayer is too much trouble for simple decisions. It isn't if the alternative could drive a wedge in your marriage. The goal of a marriage is to stay together and glorify God, not to quickly get what you want. Take the time to seek God's face together. Ask God about specific things you have heard and wonder about. I believe God will direct you when you ask Him for His guidance.

The fifth phase is the decision phase. It is called a phase because it includes the process of moving toward a decision. If, for instance, you are trying to buy a new car, there will come a time when the husband will say something like, "Honey, after all of our research and prayer, I am leaning toward this car, from this dealer, and for this much money. If you have any new information that I should know before we actually do this, let me know now." After the decision is made, sometimes there are still questions to answer and issues to address. Sometimes after all the research and discussion the decision needs to be abandoned. That, too, is a part of this phase.

Marriage Solutions and Exercises

- Make 3x5 cards with one of the five phases of a good decision on each card.
  - o Discussion phase
  - o Options Phase
  - o Counsel Phase
  - o Prayer Phase
  - o Decision Phase

- Start a discussion with your spouse, using this system.

- Are there decisions from the past in which you insisted on your own way and it proved to be wrong? Apologize.

Nurture: Communication
I feel like we don't talk enough; we are becoming strangers.

"He just won't talk to me! I'm talking, but he is not listening! He just tunes me out. So, I just gave up on an intimate marriage." Jill described the lack of interaction between her and her husband. He didn't want to engage in the kind of dialogue that was rich and fulfilling for her. She got his attention by leaving.

Steve thought they had a really good marriage. It was meeting his needs perfectly. When she fired the shot across the bow by leaving just a note, he called to see if I could help him fix his marriage. According to the Bible, a married man has a responsibility (Eph. 5:29) to nourish his wife, so she will blossom into the woman God desires her to be. The term *nourish* is a gardening term. It means, "to supply the essential nutrients needed for a plant to grow to its potential." A plant needs sunlight, water, and fertilizer. A key element almost every woman needs is conversation. It must go deeper than just surface details.

She needs a back-and-forth dialogue about her, about him, and about each of the children. Her husband needs to ask questions about her interests and thoughts. She also wants to explore his thoughts and feelings with openness and honesty. The two highest levels of friendship are close friendship and intimate friendship, and those require deep, interactive communication. There must be openness about fears, desires, anxieties, hopes, frustrations, sadness, and other feelings. When a man shuts down his communication, he may feel more comfortable, but his wife feels shut out. I am always amazed at how men are full of conversation about their feelings and difficulties when dating, but when they get married, it stops.

A husband who wants to truly love his wife must learn the skills of good listening. This means he must make and keep eye contact with her while she is talking (no reading the paper or watching TV). Good listening means he leans in and shows with his body language that he is interested in what she says. A man who nurtures his wife by listening will ask questions to learn more. He will reflect her strong emotional words and paraphrase her comments to make sure he understood what she said. He will allow the conversation to go where his wife wants it to go, rather than bring up his stories or hijacking the conversation to his topics. Being a good, romantic listener means being willing to enter into her mental point of view. That doesn't necessarily mean agreeing with her point of view. Only when a husband is willing to share his wife's thoughts and feelings can deep, nurturing love be exchanged. A husband with good listening skills will summarize to make sure the real topic is adequately explored.

Skills of an Effective Listener

There are six major skills of a good listener.

- Eye contact—focus on the speaker. That communicates interest.

- Minimal encouragers—words, phrases, groans, raised eyebrows, and nods of the head that say, "Keep talking." People need these clues to feel listened to.

- Verbal following—the listener allows the direction of conversation to be determined by the speaker. The listener doesn't redirect the topic.

- Asking questions—the listener asks questions to clarify and gently probe. The more curiosity and interest the listener conveys, the more the speaker will share.

- Summarize—the listener gives a short summary of the main points. This is a crucial way to clarify the speaker's content and to communicate a desire to really listen. If you were unclear of what the speaker meant or you misunderstood the context, the speaker will correct you.

- Insights—the listener shares insights, conclusions, connections, and reasons the speaker has not necessarily seen. Deep friendships and love are built here.

The more a person practices these skills, the better listener he or she becomes. Better listening improves marital connection. Can you imagine a woman moving away from the most effective listener in her life?

Marriage Solutions and Exercises

- Ask specific questions about the 10 major relationships in your wife's life: God, self, marriage, family, work, church, finances, society, friends, and enemies

- Whenever she asks questions about you, make sure at some point you ask a question about her. It is very easy to forget to ask questions about the other person. Don't make that mistake.

- Practice the six skills of listening.
- Recognize two types of conversation: normal and deep interaction. Your wife needs both types to feel satisfied in her marriage. She must have the normal business-type conversation about money, kids, work, etc., but she must also have a deeper conversation about dreams, goals, hopes, fears, and needs.

Nurture: Dating and Romance
I feel taken for granted instead of special and pursued.

In a moment of blunt honesty about the despair in her marriage, Elizabeth blurted out, "All you want is a maid, a mistress, and a mother to your children!" John didn't say anything but he thought to himself, "What's wrong with that?" John and Elizabeth almost lost their marriage because he didn't understand that she needed to be pursued. When John began to schedule regular dates with his wife, it marked a significant change in their marriage. In his mind he had been dating her, but the dates were six months apart or included the kids. I explained to him that Elizabeth needed him to pursue her soul every week in an improved context. He obviously knew how to pursue her body, but pursuing her soul was a new thought. "How do you do that?" he asked.

"Elizabeth is full of thoughts, emotions, ideas, dreams, fears, hopes and perspectives," I explained. "She needs you to *want* to know those things about her. Those thoughts and her personality are what make up her soul. Every week new information and experiences are added. She wants to share all of that with you. She wants you to want to pursue that knowledge. When you draw that information out of her all week, it's wonderful. Then when you take her to a nice restaurant to pursue her further, it floods her soul. That is called romance."

John made the adjustments in his schedule and more importantly in his mind. He began to love her the way she needed to be loved. Their marriage is still going strong after more than 20 years.

The Bible is clear that a husband needs to cherish and nourish his wife (Eph. 5:28-29). That means he must supply the nutrients she needs to thrive as a person. The pursuit of her soul is imperative for a woman to thrive in her marriage. Scripture also implies a woman's need for romance (Song 1:4; Eph. 5:30).

The average man has a hard time understanding why he should continue to pursue what he has already caught. Most men don't need to be romanced the way a woman does. She needs to be pursued in her soul in an improved context. An improved context means that a woman is treated nicer than in her everyday life.

In improved context there is more of a display of deference and manners. The destination is a highly enjoyable place. In many cases, that means the restaurant is fancier than the level she lives at normally. The idea here is that when a woman is romanced, she is treated better than normal. She is addressed gently and politely. Her positive qualities are identified. Her husband listens and interacts with her opinions.

She wants her husband to want to know about her. She needs him to plan to spend time with her so she can look forward to better days. It is often a revelation for a man to grasp that she gets little to nothing out of meeting your needs. She's waiting for you to meet her needs. She has a deep need to be pursued by her husband. This is a way he can prove to her that he loves her. If he is willing to go out of his way to pursue her soul in an improved context, it ministers to the deep recesses of her heart.

Marriage Solutions and Exercises

- Pick a day of the week that you can schedule a regular date with your wife.

- Prepare at least 10 questions you can ask during the date.

- Write down five potential dates you think would be fun for your wife.

Nurture: Affection and Tender Touch

I feel alone, unattractive, discouraged, ugly, and non-special.

Roger and Barbara communicated with demanding, angry tones and lots of silence in between. I asked her, "When was the last time your husband touched you and he didn't do it just to take you to the bedroom?" She looked up at the ceiling for a long time and said, "Ten years." I exclaimed, "It has been ten years since your husband touched you tenderly without sexual expectations?" "Yeah," she said, "that's about right!"

It took only a short period of time to teach Roger that holding his wife's hand and putting his arm around her were small sacrifices for him, but they paid rich dividends. He started helping her on with her coat. He was openly affectionate and tender in public. Instead of treating her like one of his colleagues at work with a shove or a punch, he began to lightly touch her and stroke her back. He learned how to give good encouraging non-sexual hugs. All of that helped to improve his marriage immediately.

Contrary to popular myth, there aren't many desperate housewives longing for sexual activity. However, there are millions of housewives desperate for affection and a tender touch from their husbands. The Bible says in 1 Corinthians 7:4 that a man's body is not his own, and he should use his body to meet the needs of his wife. She doesn't have a need for sexual intercourse. She has a need for him to caress her tenderly and cuddle with her gently without it always leading to the bedroom. For her the whole arena of affection is not the preliminaries to the main event. For most women, it *is* the main event. It's difficult for the average man to realize his wife doesn't have his strong sex drive. She is (typically) simply not interested in sex as much as he is. She does, however, have a need to be treated with tenderness and nonsexual affection.

The husband needs to demonstrate that he loves his wife with meaningful hugs, tender touches, and caresses. Most women want and need their husband to display public affection by holding hands, helping her to put on her coat, hugging, putting his arm around her, and kissing her lightly on the cheek or lips. Those are all ways a woman wants to feel special. It matters that her man is still affectionate. Those may seem like small and insignificant acts to men, but the wise man realizes his wife needs them and he richly supplies them.

Different women need different kinds of affection, so take the time to determine the specific ways your wife wants to receive affection and tender touches.

Marriage Solutions and Exercises

- Hold your wife's hand in public at least once a week.

- Sit with her and gently put your arm around her at least once a week.

- Cuddle with your wife at least once a week without having sexual intercourse.

- Learn how to softly hug your wife and hold her for 3-5 minutes in a comforting way. Work on this together if one of you is not accustomed to tender touch.

Defender

*I feel unprotected and undefended, alone in my battles,
put down, and exposed to others' attacks.*

Years ago I heard the story of a woman who was seeing a marriage counselor to help her cope with her marriage. During the course of the therapy, the counselor started flirting with her. That was unexpected, flattering, and troubling all at the same time. His advances grew stronger. After a few weeks of this, the woman received some wise counsel to inform her husband. When she did, it roused her husband out of his marital slumber to contend for his marriage. The counselor was fired, and her husband engaged in his marriage as the defender of his wife's honor and decency.

There is something in a man that wants to rally to his wife's defense when he perceives she is threatened. What most men don't realize is that most threats are not overt. He needs to defend her often because there are a number of attacks that could cripple her. When men perceive danger, they must speak up and come to her rescue.

Let us draw out of this idea of cherishing our wives a few more truths (Eph. 5:28). A husband needs to stand ready to keep various overt and subtle problems from derailing his wife's life. Everyone needs feedback to establish boundaries, gently expose blind spots, offer well-placed encouragement, give warnings, and clarify potential co-dependent behaviors. It is in those ways a husband can truly become the defender of his wife. A husband's responsibility is to make sure the seemingly small problems in life don't overwhelm her. Let me give you a few examples.

There are television shows your wife may want to see, but she can't cope with the images in her head. There are activities your wife may want to try that will introduce her to people, problems, and situations she is not prepared for. There are people who are toxic to your wife's whole mood, and she doesn't have the strength to break away from them. There may be activities that rob her of the time she needs for more important things, but she can't bring herself to say no.

As a husband you should know what stresses her out, what energizes her, and what are her areas of needed growth. Don't assume your wife is an independent superwoman who doesn't need or want your help. Also realize she has blind spots and dysfunctional areas where she needs you to come alongside to assist her. She doesn't need you to berate her or demand she change. She needs you to defend her in areas where she is weak.

Every woman is different. Because of her upbringing, temperament, skills, and desires, she has specific weaknesses where you must defend her. If she is especially fearful of robbery or fire, you must address those concerns. It doesn't help to advise her to grow out of those fears because you don't share them. You must defend her. If she has a friend who fills her with destructive ideas, it is not enough to counteract the bad ideas. You need to help her discover how to distance herself. If your wife constantly overcommits, you need to work with her to develop a balanced schedule that works long term.

For years a man blamed his wife for being overweight. He was thin and able to say no to desserts and treats. She, however, used food as an emotional comfort whenever things didn't go her way. He gave reasons why she should lose weight. He kept ragging on her to skip the desserts and treats like he did. He almost lost his marriage over the issue of her weight because he always made it her problem. If he saw her weight as an enemy attacking his wife, perhaps he could help defeat it. He eventually learned to accept her for who she was, and this allowed their marriage to heal.

What is God calling you to defend your wife from? Where is she struggling? Learn to see your wife's troubles as opportunities to be a true husband. When your wife soars above her problems because you've helped her defeat them, the whole world will know you are an example of Christ. When approached with gentleness and humility, your wife will welcome you as her defender.

Marriage Solutions and Exercises

Have a discussion with your wife about how you could defend her in these areas.

- Physical defense: Do you ever feel physically unsafe? Where?
- Defense against addictions: Are you dependent on something?
- Relational defense: Are there any toxic people in your life?
- Mental defense: Are you watching or hearing disturbing movies, music, TV, or radio shows?
- Emotional defense: Are there any situations/ people who produce fear, bitterness in you?
- Financial defense: What do you need financially?
- Organizational defense: What do you need at work to thrive?

Conclusion

If a husband really learns how to minister to the deep relational needs of his wife, he will have a marriage that satisfies the deep places of his soul. The way for a man to have everything he ever wanted in his marriage is to make sure he loves his wife as Christ loves the church. He will gain a great marriage by loving his wife before himself.

Becoming a Loving Wife

In this section, I will give an overview of the wife's role in loving her husband. In essence, this is her job description as a wife. This does not define her as a woman, but it shows her what her husband needs. In the past, most problems that ended marriages came from husbands not loving their wives, but these days more wives are experimenting with selfishness. Just like men, if wives don't meet the needs of their husbands, marriages will develop predictable diseases and may die. It is crucial that wives meet their husband's needs and thereby grow the marriage they desire.

Respect
A husband needs a wife who will respect and admire him.

It was almost impossible for Greg to resist the admiration and affection Sharon sent his way during the dating phase. She was loud, strong, and seemingly dedicated to his realization of how wonderful he was. He drank in her admiration. It didn't take long to consider marriage to a woman who constantly brought up his good points. She found it easy to admire him while they dated. Unfortunately her strong personality also found it easy to trumpet his weaknesses and mistakes once they married. Their marriage became increasingly troubled. She didn't see the connection between his emotional distance and her negative comments. He desperately tried everything to hear her sing his praises once again. Their marriage was headed for divorce. But then Greg learned how to minister to her needs, and Sharon learned how to overlook his faults and give him the respect and admiration he needed. Scripture reinforces this principle, "See to it that she respects her husband" (Eph. 5:33). *Respect* means "to acknowledge value, to admire and to appreciate." Most men decided to marry based upon the respect and admiration they received when dating. A man is drawn toward a woman who focuses on what he does well. If a woman disrespects him, he doesn't want to be near her. If a husband is never home or refuses to engage, it may be that he gets more respect from other places and, therefore, receives no benefit for involvement at home.

Respect is like air to a man. He needs to see the sparkle in his wife's eyes when she sees him. He breathes in her compliments and is energized by her admiration. Every man has areas that need improvement, but a great marriage isn't built by focusing on them. He will either work to correct the situation, or he will divorce himself from her. Realize this truth: *We all want to be with people who focus on our positives, and we avoid people who focus on our shortcomings.*

It is often difficult for a wife to focus on the positive when she sees so much room for improvement. If she allows the voids in his life to dominate her thinking, she will begin to disrespect him. That will drain the life out of the relationship and take away his energy for change. A lack of respect from his wife virtually dooms a husband to intensify his present dysfunctional patterns. He may also begin to look for people who will respect him. If he finds respect at the pool hall, the office, or a bar, he will constantly want to be there. The respect provides him emotional fuel. What many women don't realize is that he needs affirmation *every day*.

We are drawn to people who value us. When another person compliments us or notices our hard work, it creates an emotional air pocket for us to breathe. It may be an oversimplification, but to marry another person means, "I want you to tell me I'm wonderful and significant every day."

There seem to be three kinds of marriages in terms of giving and receiving value. First, there is the marriage where both husband and wife value each other with praise, attention, and celebration of each other's strengths and victories. In those marriages, couples are magnetically drawn to one another because they receive value. This value allows them to grow and accomplish far more than either could as separate individuals.

Second, there are marriages that are value neutral. In this kind of marriage the basic services of food, shelter, clothing, and conjugal visits are given but there is no focus on encouragement or notice of strengths and victories. They bump along under the title of a "good" marriage but are closer to an affair than they realize. If someone else starts showing lots of respect or admiration, an affair becomes a realistic possibility. However, they can awaken if supplied with renewed admiration, respect, and praise.

Third, there are marriages that focus on mistakes, shortcomings, and weaknesses. These marriages exist as two opposing sides, "Who is right?" and "When will you admit you were wrong?" These marriages are heading to some form of divorce: emotional, mental, physical, or actual. These people had the same marriages the people in the first category had, but they chose to focus on shortcomings, mistakes, weaknesses, and past transgressions. Everyone has negative areas, but if you focus on them, you will destroy your marriage. It can be difficult to focus on the admirable qualities and actions of your spouse, but it pays rich dividends.

Humanly speaking, your spouse is the most important possession you have. He holds the key to your life. You can choose to highly prize your husband for his good points. The more you do, the better your marriage. Does your husband know what you admire about him? Is your focus on what he does right or what he does wrong? Do you look for opportunities to praise and compliment him? Do you notice all of his victories, even the small ones? Those are actions of respect.

Marriage Solutions and Exercises

- Admire or appreciate something specific about your husband every day.

- Focus on five things he does well. Many times they will be work-related. Make sure he receives more admiration and approval from you than anyone else.

- Memorialize and display your husband's accomplishments around the house.

- Appreciate your husband's efforts even if they aren't successful.

Adaptation
*A husband needs a wife who will adapt to him
as a person, partner, and leader.*

Sarah just could not adapt to Craig. She tried and although life improved, she didn't like that she didn't always have the final say. She was very strong and independent and felt it was beneath her to have to adapt to anyone except herself. Craig and Sarah for a while attended the church I pastored. For a few years their marriage improved. He received promotions. The children felt the benefits of stability. And Sarah dealt with a host of past issues and started to build a hopeful future. But adapting to her husband rather than making him adapt to her wore thin. They tried other churches because I had said that her adapting to Craig's need was a biblical command. Eventually she gave up on her marriage and went back to the chaotic life she lived when she was boss. Craig was not a demanding man; in fact, he was very adaptable. Being adaptable has nothing to do with who is smarter, who is a better leader, or who makes more money. It has to do with harmony and need.

Both men and women must adapt to each other in their marriages. However, men are more sensitive to a lack of adaptation. A man has a high need for his wife to adapt to him and the life he builds. If he senses resistance to his ideas or leadership in the home, he will quickly distance himself from involvement in the marriage and family. He tends to give up. She may want to negotiate or request more information, but it doesn't feel that way to him. First he wants to hear her willingness to adapt, and then he'll discuss details.

The Bible several times specifically commands wives to adapt to their husbands (Eph. 5:22; 1 Peter 3:1; Col. 3:18; Titus 2:5). If God repeats this idea that often, it's important. A man needs to sense his wife is on his team and not pursuing her own agenda. If he does not, he will be tempted to spend his time away from the home and family. As a word of balance, a wife is never asked to adapt to a violation of God's moral boundaries or to a man who degrades her personhood. But I have watched wives destroy the potential of their marriage because of personal preference.

A great marriage requires adapting and compromising from both partners. If a husband stubbornly holds onto something that damages the marriage, he needs to adapt to reality. He can't do as he pleases and expect to avoid consequences. If a wife stubbornly insists on personal preferences over her husband's objections, she will reduce the joy in her marriage even if she gets her way. Her husband will withdraw leadership and energy from the relationship because he senses resistance. It doesn't take many "that's stupid" comments from his wife to know she won't adapt to his leadership. He's then tempted to run to other places where adaptation will take place.

Many women drive their husbands away because they dismiss or ridicule what makes perfect sense from a male point of view. When he brings a person home from work without warning, can she adapt? When he talks about adding a pool table or rearranging the furniture, does she allow its possibility? Is the husband's direction for parenting the children respected and incorporated? Are the husband's tastes and ideas expressed in the look and feel of the home? Remember that a man will abandon any arena where his ideas are not valued.

There has to be sufficient adaptation to his ideas for the husband to take part in this enterprise. The less adaptation of his ideas and guidance, the less of him there will be. This may be a hard truth to accept, but if a woman wants her husband to be deeply involved, then his ideas, style, likes, and temperament need to be vital to the relationship. Most men will not tolerate being emasculated just so they can be a part of their own marriage.

Marriage Solutions and Exercises

Think about the following questions:

- Does your husband think you resist his ideas or that you fail to adapt?

- If your husband had complete authority in your home, what three changes would he make? How can you make those changes?

- In what ways have you changed to make your marriage better?

- Describe five changes you could make to be a better spouse.

- What does perfect harmony and peace with your spouse look like?

Domestic Leadership
A husband needs a wife who will exercise domestic leadership.

There is a need rarely spoken of in our culture because it's not politically correct. A man needs to have a wife who will exercise her leadership skills to run the home and family. This idea has become taboo so that most people are unwilling to talk about it. But the testimony of Scripture and modern psychology is that men have a deep need for their wives to exercise strong leadership in their homes.

It is not the only area where women can exercise leadership gifts, but husbands desperately need their wives to make it a priority. If a wife is a corporate president or runs a charity but gives little time and energy to the domestic side of her marriage and family, something dies inside her husband.

Meredith did not realize she was destroying her marriage by expecting her husband to do 50 percent of everything around the house. Meredith called me after I had been working with her husband, David, for about a year. He had made a 180-degree turnaround to become the loving husband she hoped he would be. His turnaround made her admit that her lack of leadership and involvement in the home had been a major factor in their separation. She told me, "I just didn't step up to my responsibility as a wife and mother. I wanted everything done for me. I believed the lie that it could all go my way without me putting in some effort. We could've avoided so much pain and hurt if I had been what I should've been."

Marriage requires incredible amounts of leadership from both parties, especially if you are blessed with children. When one of the partners withdraws his or her leadership skills, ideas, talents, or gifting from the marriage, it will obviously achieve less than its fullest potential. In modern culture it has become normal for most men to ignore leadership responsibilities in the marriage and family. Now it is more typical for a woman also to withdraw her leadership component from the marriage and family. That is tragic, and it results in dissolved marriages and devastated children.

The Bible declares that a husband must bring his leadership gifts and talents to the marriage and family (Eph. 5:22; 1 Cor. 11:3; 1 Tim. 3:4, 5). It also says a wife must bring her leadership gifts and talents to the marriage and family (Titus 2:5; 1 Tim. 5:14). Her leadership and focus are needed for her marriage to produce well-adjusted kids.

An orderly family and well maintained home is the goal, but that doesn't mean the woman does all the work. Enlisting the kids and outside help, as well as a doable honey-do list, is entirely appropriate. A man's heart is drawn home when he knows his wife has exercised her leadership to either handle the problems or create possible solutions for them to discuss. She is not helpless; she is motivated to see her home, marriage, and children thrive. When a woman uses her skills to plan and delegate like a leader, everybody wins.

Marriage Solutions and Exercises

- Does your husband think of your home as an inviting place?
- Discuss changes needed in your home for order and beauty.
- What is needed for your children to be well-behaved, productive members of society?
- Discuss, "What do we want our family to be like in five years?"

Intimacy

*A husband needs a wife who will joyfully
meet his consistent need for physical intimacy.*

Jill made some changes and saved her marriage. Her husband, Reuben, had moved into an apartment near his workplace. He was on his way out of the marriage. He gave her a long list of things wrong in their marriage. She could no longer do anything about some of the items on the list, but two items caught her attention. She wasn't interested in sex anymore, and she had become an unattractive mom. For the sake of her marriage and her children, Jill stopped focusing on her lack of interest in sex and focused instead on his interest in it. When Reuben was ready, Jill was ready. She even started initiating intimacy before he expected it. If this were his number one relational need, she would meet it before some floozy from the office could. She changed her appearance from dowdy mom to attractive young wife. These changes certainly caught Reuben's attention. He spent less time at the new apartment and more time at his house. Eventually he stopped going to the apartment because he had an attractive woman waiting at his home. Jill rescued her marriage, and her boys got their father back because she committed herself to meet his number one need. Many changes were still needed to make their marriage work long-term, but she clearly had his attention. He knew his attractive wife would meet his number one need.

Both men and women have the need for sexual intercourse, but the need is clearly higher in men in most cases. For years men have complained that God gave their wives a monthly cycle. Every month she has a period, and her emotions are heightened. She has a biological, 28-day cycle in which she is interested in sexual activity during a short period of time—usually at the climax of her fertility.

Many women don't understand that men also have a cycle. Every two to five days a man has a build-up of sperm that needs to be released. The average man produces about 100-200 million sperm every 24 hours. When the number reaches 400-500 million, there is a physiological need to release those sperm. About this time, everything begins to take on a sexual tone. His whole body is rallying to make the conditions right to get rid of those sperm. Women who aren't aware of this cycle believe their husband is sex-crazed because he wants it all the time.

"He just had it the other day, and he's asking to fool around again! Doesn't he ever get enough?" No. It is a constantly renewed need.

Sex is usually listed as number one in terms of what a man relationally needs from his wife. If a wife desires marital intelligence, she will understand his need for sexual release and fulfill it. Embrace the fact of it, even if this is not your feminine reality. When I have talked to women who resent this need in their husbands, I ask, "How much time does it take you to meet this need?"

"Ten to fifteen minutes," is the usual reply. "Never more than a half an hour." At this point I ask, "Then is it too much trouble to spend 10 to 15 minutes every few days to meet your husband's number one need?" Usually I get all kinds of defensive excuses. That tells me that meeting this need is more about how they think sexuality should be expressed rather than what their husbands need. Many women think it should be a monthly planned encounter preceded by lots of talking, cuddling, and slow foreplay. While this idealized encounter has much to commend it, there are some problems with it. It is almost the perfect expression of a woman's physiological response to her own sexual hormones and cycle. Both husbands and wives have different ideas of the right way to be together sexually.

Both ideas come from their own physiology or past experience. It is possible to incorporate both visions of sexual intimacy into a marriage but only if the wife is willing to meet her husband's need for more frequent sexual encounters.

Some men put unrealistic demands on their wives to respond quickly and enthusiastically to all their sexual advances. Calm discussion and gentle suggestions will make for a mutually enjoyable sex life. When a wife ministers to her husband in the sexual arena, it strengthens his ability to fight off attractions to affairs, pornography, and other sexual temptations. When a man has a wife who is a consistent enthusiastic sexual partner, he is encouraged in his marriage and usually willing to learn how to meet her needs.

Marriages usually need at least three different kinds of sexual relations. First, they need at least once a month a sexual encounter where both are really excited. Second, they need a weekly method of having sex that is mutually satisfying. Third, the couple will need to find a mutually acceptable way of sexual release without full engagement of the wife.

Marriage Solutions and Exercises

- Initiate sexual intimacy with your husband twice this week.
- Describe three different ways to have romantic sexual relations with your spouse.
- Describe three different ways to have a quick sexual encounter with your spouse.

Companionship
A husband needs a wife who will learn to enjoy
spending time in his favorite activities.

Dawn's marriage once suffered from monotony and boredom. For many years she wouldn't take part in what Greg wanted to try. Once she was willing to discover new things and experience new places, his love for her soared. When she attended a football game, traveled to an out-of-the-way place and attended a seminar he found fascinating, his love for her went way up. When Dawn suggested she wanted to try all kinds of things he enjoyed, it enlivened their marriage.

Some of men's greatest joys are hobbies, adventures, or job assignments. If his wife is with him when he is experiencing these joys, he associates joy with her. Her physical presence in the midst of what he finds satisfying increases his love for her.

Both men and women want a deep friendship with their spouse. For men this means that his wife shares common activities and becomes his companion. For women it means deep conversation and shared feelings and needs. A husband longs for his wife to join him in his pursuits and interests. He wants her to be fascinated by what fascinates him. Men see a companion as someone who shares a common interest. It is a side-by-side relationship in which two people enjoy something together. Recent studies suggest this natural orientation for side-by-side relationships may be linked to the fact that men have more rods in their eyes. They are drawn to motion and action. That requires that their friends stand by their sides.[4]Women, on the other hand, are universally invested with more cones, which are drawn to detail and bright colors. That may explain a greater interest in face-to-face communication and interaction.[5]This is what builds friendship. Women usually want to move past the common interest to share deep needs and feelings. Men don't necessarily need to share deep feelings—often the common interest is enough. Men usually list companionship as the second highest need in their marriage and a significant reason to get married. They want to be with someone doing things they enjoy.

God makes it clear in the Scriptures that a truly loving wife will learn to love her husband in the way of a friend (Titus 2:4, Gen. 2:18). God doesn't give commands that happen naturally, so the instruction for wives to love their husbands seems strange. The word for love in these passages is built on the root word *phileo*, which means "friendship, companion-type love." This side-by-side love is often difficult for wives to embrace. The interests of men are very different from the interests of women. A wise woman learns how to be her husband's companion. Just as your husband learns to engage you in conversation not naturally fascinating to him, learn to embrace the joys of your husband's interests.

What common interests do you and your spouse enjoy? The more these mutual activities are developed, the more joy in the marriage. Explore new activities together. Realize a man is drawn to a woman who invests time and energy in what he finds interesting. One marriage counselor suggests spouses avoid any hobby or activity that doesn't include an immediate family member.[6]

Marriage Solutions and Exercises

- Schedule recreational time at least once a month doing something you both enjoy.

- See Appendix 3 for recreation ideas you could pursue with your spouse.

- Ask your spouse what he/she likes to do.

- Plan a new activity both of you are interested in.

Attractive Soul and Body

*A husband needs a wife who will maintain
her outward appearance and develop an attractive soul.*

Cindy let herself go. She was at least 100 pounds overweight and no longer attended to her looks. She came to see me when her husband had an affair. "How could he do this to me?" she moaned. Most instructive was the person with whom her husband was having an affair. He had an affair with a woman even more overweight than Cindy. "Why would he have an affair with *her*?" she shrieked. Finally, she was told. "Yes, this other woman was overweight, but her personality, gratefulness, charm, and inner beauty made her a joy to be with." The other woman also did the best she could with her make-up, hair, and clothes. Cindy could have handled his affair with an attractive young floozy more easily. But a woman who was also overweight? It was a slap in the face for how critical, demanding, negative, and ungrateful she had become.

Cindy's lack of inner beauty was exposed. Far more important than letting herself go physically was her having become ugly on the inside. Instead of developing gratefulness, charm, gentleness, and inner beauty to win her husband back, she got mad, bitter, and even more critical. When her friends tried to help her understand what was really going on in her marriage, she refused to believe that her own critical and cynical demeanor had anything to do with his affair. Her bitterness destroyed her marriage and friendships. She refused to deal with reality. After spewing venomous insults at those she knew, she skipped town.

The Scriptures and thousands of years of male interaction with women say the same thing. Men are drawn to beautiful women but are even more magnetized by an attractive woman with an attractive soul. 1 Peter 3:3-4 says, "Your adornment must not be merely external—braiding the hair, and wearing gold jewelry, or putting on dresses; but let it be the hidden person of the heart, with the imperishable quality of a gentle and quiet spirit, which is precious in the sight of God." A beautiful woman who lacks inner beauty quickly loses her appeal. No one wants to spend time with a selfish, critical, whiny person no matter how good-looking she may be.

A man needs to connect with a woman who has an attractive body and an increasingly attractive soul. As in the story above, attractiveness is in the eye of the beholder. Most men aren't looking for movie-star looks—just a wife who takes care of herself. A key to a happy marriage for a man is a wife with growing inner beauty that completely overshadows physical flaws and the effects of aging. A man is attracted by physical beauty, but connection happens with a woman who is pleasant, grateful, nonjudgmental, forgiving, and respectful. Culture puts incredible pressure on women to achieve an unattainable standard of external beauty. This is to keep cash registers ringing throughout the beauty industry. Men are usually less demanding in terms of physical attractiveness than women are. If a man marries a woman he found physically attractive, he expects her to remain attractive outwardly, but his greater need is for internal beauty.

External attractiveness through clothing, hair, make-up, and weight control are important. If you have allowed yourself to be less than your best in these areas, take the time and energy to improve. Don't neglect to take care of yourself and expect him to love you anyway. Just like your husband needs to go to work when he doesn't feel like it or listen when he may not be interested, you need to put in the work to remain physically attractive to him. Don't be discouraged if you need time to change. Losing weight doesn't happen overnight! Stay with it—you're working toward a great marriage, and he'll appreciate your effort.

All people age, and the flower of their outer beauty withers. However, if the soul grows in gratefulness, forgiveness, respect, friendliness, and deference (among other qualities), inner beauty shines through. No one is drawn to a harsh, selfish, and deprecating spouse. Those qualities push people away and destroy a marriage's potential. It is difficult to live with a person 24/7 and still focus on his/her good points, but your marriage requires it. Many seem to save the worst behavior for those closest to them. That is foolish. We see headlines of beautiful movie stars who marry and then divorce because they are selfish, egocentric people who demand pampering by those around them. As you grow older, commit yourself to becoming a deeper, richer, more generous person. It will attract a lot of good things, including your husband.

Marriage Solutions and Exercises

- Increase the beauty of your soul through generosity, gratefulness, forgiveness, deference, encouragement, and optimism.

- Plan ways to remain physically attractive: clothing, hair, make-up, and weight.

- Apologize for times of relational ugliness.

- Apologize to your spouse once every two weeks even if you think it isn't necessary.

- Thank your spouse for putting up with you.

Listening

A husband needs a wife who will listen to him unpack his soul.

In a men's discussion group, I quickly outlined one of the major problems in marriages. Wives will often not listen to what a husband is feeling or dreaming about because its results are threatening or unwanted. I barely explained the concept before a man emphatically finished the sentence saying, "That makes her not a safe person!" Ed explained that this is what he repeatedly told his wife. He felt if she didn't listen to his story and feelings without reaction, she wasn't a safe person, and, therefore, he stopped talking. He went on to tell us his wife didn't understand that, so he no longer shared anything of depth with her. How tragic that Ed's wife was denied something she wanted most from her marriage. And it was her fault.

Many wives inadvertently shut down the very intimate communication they crave. Men need their wives to help them talk out their emotions, plans, frustrations, possible solutions, and ideas. It isn't usually interactive communication but rather a deep trip into his soul. He always checks to see if she is listening with affirmation and patience. Because the wife hears things very personally, it may be too much for her to handle when he talks of dreams, fantasies, struggles, or temptations. She immediately pictures herself living in Montana operating a trout farm, or trying to make ends meet if he quits his job, or raising the kids alone because he has given in to a temptation. Because she hears things through the grid of what it means to her, she may tune him out when he wants to talk about those thoughts. If a wife refuses to listen to her husband's deep ramblings three to five times consecutively, he'll conclude she's not a safe person. As a result, her dream of intimacy is over. He needs her to listen to his heart even if it is bombastic, fearful, boring, or repetitive. He reveals and discovers himself through these conversations.

A man's emotions are buried in a different part of the brain than a woman's.[7] Science now tells us a woman stores her emotions in the same place her verbal center operates, so she is very aware of her emotions and can describe them quickly and accurately.[8] Studies show a man stores his emotions deep in his brain with few neural pathways to his verbal center. While he has just as many emotions as a woman, he is less aware of them and can't describe them as easily.[9] He has less access to these aspects of his soul and has a harder time understanding his emotions and their power. Therefore he repeats his stories and continues to mull over his irritations to get a lock on their meaning and significance.

Most men would never admit it, but they perceive talking with their spouse much like a visit to a psychologist. They want to talk while she listens with rapt attention, asking relevant questions with no emotional reactions. After sufficient trust is built, the wife can provide insight. Men repeatedly return to the same relationships, incidents, and situations for reassurance. It is through these conversations that men express emotions they have difficulty verbalizing.

Men want their wives to be a "lightning rod" who can draw away the raw electricity of the emotions they feel. A man longs to have a woman who is able to draw out his thoughts and emotions without judgment. There must be a level of trust and guaranteed comfort that will continue when the conversation ends.

The soul of a human being is a fearful and wonderful place. Our souls are full of dreams, fears, desires, emotions, vulnerabilities, hopes, and memories. They can be wonderful, yet troubling. No one lets another into the darkest places of the soul easily. It takes time and trust. Repeated periods of nonjudgmental listening and continued acceptance are required before the hidden treasures of the soul are exposed.

Every husband wants to let his wife into his soul, but many women can't handle this privilege. They disqualify themselves by recoiling, interrupting, changing the subject, or judging. Becoming the intimate friend of a man requires a level of emotional and mental sobriety that comes only from the Spirit of God. I believe that is why the Bible tells women to grow in this area (1 Tim. 3:11; Titus 2:4). Our wives must understand our souls are not safe. There are all kinds of scary thoughts, memories, and emotions that inhabit them (Jer. 17:9). But if we can share this side of ourselves with safe people, we won't act on those impulses. The person who can weaken inclinations, emotions, and schemes through conversation is safest. It is the people we allow into our souls that make the biggest impact. The key to this level of influence is nonjudgmental listening.

Read these ancient biblical truths on the importance and power of a wife's ability to listen. I have included a longer passage in 1 Peter 3:1-4 because it incorporates ideas about helping husbands and bringing about positive change in their lives. I have added emphasis to reinforce my point.

In the same way, you wives, be submissive to your own husbands so that even if any of them are disobedient to the word, *they may be won without a word by the behavior of their wives*, as they observe your chaste and respectful behavior. Your adornment must not be merely external—braiding the hair, and wearing gold jewelry, or putting on dresses; *but let it be the hidden person of the heart, with the imperishable quality of a gentle and quiet spirit*, which is precious in the sight of God.

It is very important there be no condemnation on what the husband shares—at least initially. The journey of moral self-discovery can come later through well-placed questions like: "Do you think that was helpful?" "How did that make you feel?" "What are the consequences?" "How does this square up with what you understand to be right?" It is essential to demonstrate a willingness to listen to your husband's feelings, even if they're disturbing. He is similar to a little boy coming to his mother with hopes she will listen to his whole story and then take his side. He has a perspective and doesn't want objectivity; usually he wants reinforcement. He will allow correction only if he has received acceptance first.

It is difficult when you hear an incorrect perspective. He doesn't want to accept a new idea that may require change or adjust a cherished point of view. To be a good listener you must follow the speaker into his mental point of view, seeking to understand his heart. Gentle questions that lead to personal breakthroughs are the most effective listening skills. It is better to listen thoroughly than to immediately correct a faulty point of view. There are times when correcting a bad perspective is essential, but that is best achieved by thorough listening.

Two words of balance are appropriate here. First, there are times when it is best to see a counselor to express certain thoughts, feelings, or memories. Because of the lack of personal involvement, a third party doesn't have to battle emotions, internal conclusions, and reactive scheming.

Second, a man who has concluded his wife is not a safe person will still send up a trial balloon about once a year to see if anything has changed. If she has improved as a listener, he will share a little more. If she again shuts him down in some way, he will return to his non-communicative shell.

Marriage Solutions and Exercises

- Practice the skills of a good listener with others: eye contact, body lean, minimal encouragers, verbal following, asking questions, summarizing.

- Set aside an hour this week to listen to your husband. Make sure you are prepared to probe into his normal conversation. Set it up to be either side-by-side or face-to-face, whichever will allow your husband to open up.

- Take a walk with your spouse and ask questions about the ten relationships in his life: God, self, marriage, family, work, church, money, society, friends, and enemies.

- What does your husband want to talk about? Listen past the usual complaints and irritations. Ask questions about people or situations that will make him think.

Summary of the Problem of Ignoring Needs

It is important for those who know us to continue loving us. The fuel that enables marriage to work is active love—meeting needs, pursuing, and pleasing. Marriage involves a commitment before God and others to love each other no matter what life brings. That requires each one to meet the deep relational needs of the other. If those needs are not met, there will be some form of divorce—emotional, psychological, financial, or physical.

When your spouse wants to meet your deepest relational needs, you experience the height of joy. Partners count on each other to meet their needs and to forever continue the "I-feed-you-and-you-feed-me" dance. Eventually one partner will cut back the relational food the other person needs to thrive but will still expect to receive his or her share. Most people don't even realize what they've done. To get your marriage back on track, both partners must meet each other's needs and pursue and please one another.

A marriage will not grow stronger, more exciting, or more captivating until there is more love flowing between husband and wife. If your marriage is in trouble, at least one partner must kick-start a new effort to meet needs, pursue, and please. If you and/or your spouse decide you will meet each other's deepest relational needs, your marriage will improve dramatically. This will require sacrifice and redirection, but it'll be worth it.

Some marriages are in such difficulty that at least one partner is doubtful the marriage will make it or that it is worth any effort to try. If one or both partners apologize for the hurts and wounds of the past, it can open up new possibilities. That is why the next chapter is so crucial.

The Five Problems of Marriage

Ignoring Needs	Immature Behaviors	Clashing Temperaments	Competing Relationships	Past Baggage
Wife's Needs				
Honor				
Understanding				
Security				
Building Unity				
Agreement				
Nurture				
Defender				
Husband's Needs				
Respect				
Adaptation				
Domestic Leadership				
Intimacy				
Companionship				
Attractive Soul and Body				
Listener				

Problem #2

Immature Behaviors

Problem #2

Immature Behaviors

Proverbs 14:12; Philippians 2:1-3;
1 Corinthians 13:11; Ephesians 5:1-4, 8-10

Overview

John thought his sarcasm was clever and funny. At work he was considered the life of the party. At home, he continued cutting and jabbing at Ellen with his trademark witty repartee. It was all in good fun, he told himself, until she left. I got a call from John to ask me to convince his wife to return. When I called her, she sobbed into the phone, "I can't stand the constant mocking, put-downs, and snide comments about everything!" She continued, "He makes jokes about everything—my weight, the food, the house, the kids. You name it, he makes sarcastic comments about it!" By this time, she was spitting out the words, barely hiding her contempt for the man she married ten years earlier. "There is never anything positive. There are never any kind or loving words. There is never any praise."

The amazing thing is that Ellen's leaving took John completely by surprise. He saw himself as a great husband. He saw his sarcastic remarks as humorous, even though he knew most of his comments also hid the negative things that he was trying to communicate to his wife. Any time she asked whether he meant the put-down he had hurled at her, he retreated behind the mask of "No, I was just joking." Eventually her love for John died of a thousand little cuts.

She finally took what she thought was permanent action. It would be better to be alone with the kids and struggling to make ends meet than to listen to his sarcasm anymore. She would not be put down again. She'd rather be alone.

It took me a long time to convince John that his "humor" was destroying their marriage. He was being selfish and immature. It was time for him to grow up. He and his wife had not had a real conversation in years because he would not stop hiding behind sarcastic comebacks. After ten years, Ellen was done.

I didn't even try to convince her to return to John at that point. I knew she really loved him, but she couldn't handle being verbally abused any more. I spent all my time working with John to stop being sarcastic, grow up, and genuinely praise his wife for all the good things about her. I even subjected him to his own kind of humor. He didn't like having his flaws made into jokes. I was able to convince him he had a chance to repair his marriage if he tried a new way of relating to his wife. He needed to treat Ellen with honor and value her as his most prized possession at home.

"Ellen needs you to compliment her hard work and notice other positive qualities. She needs to hear that she's beautiful," I told him. "And although it may not be as much fun, you need to do it without jokes or humor. She is so wounded by your sarcasm; she waits for the punch line every time you open your mouth."

He didn't understand how Ellen could be so upset with the "life of the party" that she no longer wanted anything to do with him. But he had tried all of his proven methods and was finally willing to listen. It took three months of playing it straight and valuing her directly before she would move back home. It took more than six months before she believed it would be permanent and unpacked the last suitcase. They stayed together and worked through the issues of how to love each other. It was worth it for John to learn a new kind of humor. Sarcasm is just one of the immature behaviors that must be avoided in order to build a strong and vibrant marriage.

The second component of Marital Intelligence is avoiding and eliminating immature behaviors. Many marriages do not survive because one or both partners cling to immature and/or manipulative behaviors instead of learning how to have mature discussions and to make reasonable compromises. For a marriage to be filled with love and joy, the husband and the wife must learn to set aside immaturity no matter what is happening. The mature person has honest, encouraging, even hard conversations with his or her partner without fighting or manipulating. It is not easy to be mature when your partner is being immature, but it is essential.

Numerous books have detailed various manipulative, immature, and defensive behaviors that people use when they face difficulty, obstacles, or resistance. John Powell in *Why Am I Afraid to Tell You Who I Am?* lists 35 manipulative or hiding behaviors.[1] It is only natural that we bring these behaviors into our marriage and use them on our spouse when things are not going our way.

Raising your marital IQ requires eliminating immature behaviors as much as possible and dealing with your partner in mature ways. There seem to be three levels of immaturity in a marriage relationship.

Level 1 immature behaviors are the personal immaturities that are a part of everyone's life. They often come as a shock after the wedding: He doesn't pick up his clothes; she constantly interrupts; he has to control the TV remote; she is always late; he belches or passes gas; she has a huge interest in gossip or negative information; he gets really angry when he doesn't get his way; she gets very moody and sensitive, etc.

Level 2 immature behaviors are those actions that are specifically aimed at your marriage partner either for punishment or to gain control. We will focus on the most common of these immature behaviors in the pages ahead.

Level 3 immature behaviors are highly destructive and can permanently change a relationship or a life with just one involvement. They would include adultery, drug use, criminal behavior, violence, drunkenness, etc.

"There is a way which seems right to a man [or woman], But its end is the way of death" (Prov. 14:12). We have all learned immature ways of dealing with things we don't like, and we are tempted to use them. They are techniques to get our own way, to deflect the discussion, or to punish our spouse. If we do not grow beyond our immature behavior patterns, our marriages will never become enjoyable relationships.

Let me give you a listing of the most common immature behaviors in marriage:

S	A	D
Sarcasm/slander	Accusations/Blame	Denial
Silence	Anger	Demands
Spending	Abusive Behavior	Dishonesty
Sick/Sleep	Addiction	Depression
Stupid/Irrational	Apathy	Disrespect
Selfish	Adultery	Destruction
	Annoying Behavior	Distance/Divorce

It is not enough just to point out immature behaviors. It is important to explain the basic actions of a mature person in order to see the absolute difference between immaturity and maturity. It is not that mature people do not have problems in their marriages. The mature people at times may even be the cause of the problems, but they handle problems differently than immature people do. Mature people have honest conversations about problems, but they stay encouraging rather than blaming or tearing down their spouse. They do not continue in immature behavior, but they stop to apologize for their actions. Mature people do not react to their partner's immature behavior with their own immaturity. They are willing to be corrected. They are willing to hear perspectives other than their own. Mature people let their spouses finish their statements, topics, and ideas without attacking at every possible opportunity. They apologize for wrongs they commit. They confront immature behavior so the relationship is not damaged. Mature people love more in the face of immaturity. They make thoughtful requests instead of emotional demands. They work on eliminating their own immature behaviors. Mature people are tolerant, patient, and accepting.

The goal of this section is to help you and your partner eliminate as much immaturity from your marriage as possible. This section also will enable you to avoid being pulled into your spouse's immature behaviors and to stay focused on having mature interactions and making mature decisions.

Eight basic solutions will give you new strategies for interacting with your spouse and keeping the marriage moving forward. Too often one immature behavior leads to another, which leads to conflict or withdrawal. The immaturity, if continued, will short-circuit any marriage no matter how much you love each other. In some cases, it is not that there is not enough love in your marriage, but it is that there are too many games being played to care whether your spouse loves you. The immaturity drowns out the love.

No one should receive better treatment than our spouse. When we agreed to marry, we signed a contract that our spouse would be number one. There will be times when being positive with our spouse is the last thing we want to do, but we must keep the long-term goal of a good relationship in mind.

Being married can reveal how self-absorbed we are. If either husband or wife pursues his or her own selfish agenda exclusively without regard for the other person, the marriage is headed for trouble. There are two people in the marriage, and both need to be winning, not just one.

Immature behaviors are a fact of life. Therefore, it is important to learn the eight solutions to immature behaviors.

1. Stop being immature any longer for any reason.
2. Understand how to repair the damage through a true and effective apology.
3. Have alignment conversations before problems and misunderstanding take place.
4. Make calm, thoughtful requests of your spouse rather than cryptic messages or angry rants.
5. Cover the problem through active loving.
6. Find a way to change offending behaviors.
7. Have a hard, clarifying conversation with your spouse about the consequences of continued immature behavior.
8. Have patience, allowing God and others to influence the behavior.

Marital Intelligence Test

This test probes the actions necessary to have a great marriage. Do not be surprised by the results. Celebrate your strengths, and work on improving your weak areas. Your spouse might respond differently to the same questions. These areas of differences are opportunities to grow and improve your marriage. Hopefully, this test will whet your appetite for the solutions in this book.

Problem #2 0 = Never; 1 = Rarely; 2 = Occasionally; 3 = Sometimes; 4 = Usually; 5 = Always	
I avoid doing things I know annoy or damage my spouse.	0 1 2 3 4 5
I have calm, thoughtful conversations with my spouse about areas of concern rather than forcing him or her to guess.	0 1 2 3 4 5
I eliminate selfish or destructive behaviors that could be harmful.	0 1 2 3 4 5
I admit when I am wrong and apologize effectively.	0 1 2 3 4 5
I am open to correction and direction about actions, activities, and people that damage our marriage.	0 1 2 3 4 5
I listen when my spouse is pointing out something I have done wrong.	0 1 2 3 4 5
I am willing to grow and change to improve my marriage.	0 1 2 3 4 5
I realize that my marriage will have trouble, and I will need to apologize.	0 1 2 3 4 5
I try to understand my spouse's point of view rather than increase my intensity to get my way.	0 1 2 3 4 5
I align my expectations with my spouse ahead of time about schedules, plans, and actions.	0 1 2 3 4 5

When I feel angry with my spouse, I try to love him/her more effectively by meeting his/her needs rather than scolding, correcting, or distancing myself.	0 1 2 3 4 5
I make changes that my spouse thinks will help our marriage.	0 1 2 3 4 5
I have had hard conversations with my spouse about improvements needed in our marriage.	0 1 2 3 4 5
I am patient with my spouse's areas of weakness, allowing God time to make changes.	0 1 2 3 4 5
My spouse avoids things that annoy or irritate me.	0 1 2 3 4 5
My spouse tells me directly when he/she is angry with me rather than in another indirect way.	0 1 2 3 4 5
My spouse eliminates destructive behaviors that could destroy our marriage.	0 1 2 3 4 5
My spouse admits when he/she is wrong and truly apologizes.	0 1 2 3 4 5
My spouse is gracious, adaptable, and defers whenever possible.	0 1 2 3 4 5
My spouse listens and makes changes when I point out something he/she has done wrong.	0 1 2 3 4 5
My spouse is willing to grow and change to make our marriage better.	0 1 2 3 4 5
My spouse does not expect our marriage to be perfect and is willing to admit he/she is wrong.	0 1 2 3 4 5
My spouse tries to understand my point of view rather than walking away or becoming angry.	0 1 2 3 4 5
My spouse has had hard conversations with me about how he/she really feels about our marriage.	0 1 2 3 4 5
My spouse works hard at loving me even when I am hard to love.	0 1 2 3 4 5

My spouse initiates the alignment of our expectations about schedules, plans, and potential actions.	0 1 2 3 4 5
Subtotal Section #2	

Add up your total. How did you do? Remember that these results reflect the current condition of your relationship. Realize, too, that no one is the perfect spouse. You both have weak areas and difficulties in the journey of marriage. But with time and effort, your marriage can improve. The solutions in this book *will* work.

The positive statements on the test outline a high standard of how we should treat one another. Start applying those truths, and your relationship will improve right away.

Scoring

130 - 98: You have a very good marriage in this area. Keep it up. Have a discussion with your spouse about how to make sure you are not wounding or hurting each other.

97 - 65: You have a good marriage that could be significantly improved by avoiding selfish, angry, or destructive behaviors. Pick one thing you will stop and one new solution method discussed in this chapter that you will focus on this next month.

64 - 33: There are some serious deficiencies in your marriage. Both of you feel you are being damaged in your marriage by the actions of your spouse. You need to focus on meeting each other's relational needs at a new level and eliminating one destructive behavior. Remember your marriage will not improve until there is more love flowing between husband and wife. A good marriage is not an absence of conflict but an abundance of love.

32 - 0: There is a lack of love but significant selfishness in your marriage. It takes only one person in the marriage to make a difference in the beginning. Schedule a meeting with a counselor or pastor. You need help to increase the love and stop the damage.

Typical Immature Behaviors

Sarcasm/Ridicule/Slander

This is immature behavior that consists of correcting your spouse through witty comments: trying to be funny at your spouse's expense; making your spouse look inferior, uninformed, or stupid on a subject; refusing to give real compliments. When men lose an argument or feel they are not winning, they will often become sarcastic to change the subject or score a few points. When someone is being sarcastic, realize that it is more about him or her than about you. It often means the person is unable to have a mature conversation about difficult subjects or about issues in which he or she may be wrong or misinformed. It can also take the form of, "Let me tell you about the stupid things my spouse did." Both men and women can play this parlor game, but it is a favorite of women who feel they cannot say anything directly to their husbands.

Silence

It may be simply not talking to your spouse, speaking in short staccato sentences, and/or only speaking about functional issues or topics. In many marriages, it is the favorite form of punishment. "I just won't speak to him until he realizes how unreasonable he is being." This practice throws down egg shells all over the house, and everybody is trying not to upset the silent one anymore. It is so immature. Instead of being silent, just talk about what you thought was unfair. Realize that you will not win every argument, nor are you right all the time. The silent treatment does not help the marriage progress; it only helps your vengeful spirit and bitterness. It is destructive. It can also result in not being willing to listen to your mate regarding anything of substance.

Spending

This immature behavior results in purchasing unneeded items to salve a wounded ego, buying things clearly beyond the budget, and in making purchases before your mate has the chance to spend the money. This particular form of immaturity used to be the practice of women, but now men are doing it at an alarming rate. Purchasing a dress or gadget that the family can't afford does not help the marriage. It will eventually hurt the relationship either financially or relationally. One does not help one's marriage by salving the pain of the last interaction with a purchase, but many people every day are trying to survive their marriage this way. I am aware of one woman who had a closet full of clothes she never wore, just because the only way to deal with her marriage was to go to the mall and buy something. The woman was changed as her husband started loving her at a new level, which allowed her to face her immature behavior.

Sick/Sleep

This immature behavior chooses to handle wounds, offenses, or losses by distancing from the offending party by sleeping or being sick. In some cases this behavior pattern has become so natural that the person no longer needs to fake the sickness or sleepiness. The sick/sleep form of hiding from mature conversation has many variations, but it is essentially a way of hiding from real issues, punishing one's spouse in a way he/she can't fight back, or deflecting the emotional pain to a physical one. I am amazed at how many times such sicknesses or tiredness clear up when people get their way or when a mature conversation takes place. I remember working with one woman who told me she slept up to 16 hours a day at one point in order to cope with her marriage.

Stupid/Irrational

Irrational actions that are out of character for an individual or are disproportionate to the situation can be regarded as stupid. Such would be a partner's announcement that he is going to get a divorce because his wife didn't do what he wanted. Or, it may be the person has an affair to get back at his or her spouse for some perceived slight. It isn't that the adulterer likes the other party. He's had the affair just to punish the spouse. In another example, it may be the man who resorts to gun violence because his wife has said she will leave. Or, maybe it's the woman who wrecks her husband's cherished car because she is mad at him.

Selfish

This immature behavior is the underlying destructive element in all immature behaviors. It's all about *me*. The underlying impulse in all sin is selfishness. "I want what I want and I will get it." The deeper this self-seeking controls a person, the more immature and foolish his behavior. All of us must learn to deny our selfishness if we are going to have good to great relationships. What we want comes to us from loving, giving, ministering to others, not from grasping, demanding and manipulating. Learning to minister to others and make thoughtful requests about our own needs is called maturity.

Selfishness can be expressed on a number of levels. The first is seen when an individual does something only for himself or herself with no thought of how it will affect anyone else. Most of us are guilty of having done thoughtless, even damaging things, because we did not think about how our actions would impact someone else. On a second level, selfishness can be increasingly destructive when an individual wants something for himself or herself, realizing that other people will be hurt, harmed, or wounded by it, but doing it anyway. This is the "I don't care about you; I want what I want" attitude. It is a deeper level of selfishness when you know another person will be damaged by your action and you do it anyway. On a third level, selfishness can consume people to the point that they want what they want at a particular moment even if it will destroy others, themselves, and significant possessions, institutions, or relationships. On this level of selfishness one is consumed by a destructive impulse and makes a choice to give into that impulse even knowing what damage will happen.

Accusations/Blame

Spouses may fling charges at their partner because they are losing an argument, so they make accusations. They begin to blame their spouse for all the things going wrong in their life. No responsibility is taken for actions; it is always the other person who caused the problem. I remember one man blaming his wife for his failures at work because she did not send him off every day with positive encouragement and a kiss. Just like in junior high, it is possible for people to twist logic around to find a reason why it is all their parents' fault. Someone said, "Blaming your spouse for the stuff in your marriage is to be-lame."

Anger

There are many people who are used to getting their own way by exhibiting some form of anger. They have found it to be a weapon that enables them to win. While anger often does help a person win or punish others, it is destructive to the marriage relationship. Anger should be avoided, not unleashed on those who are closest to us. Anger is an emotional reaction to not having our expectations met. It is natural to feel strongly when our expectations are blocked, ignored, denied, resisted, or destroyed. This emotional feeling is like a live electrical wire flowing through our body. We always have the choice whether we are going to grab that wire and allow that surge of emotion to take over our body. It is immature to grab the wire and use those emotions and actions to punish our spouse or to win the argument through the display of raw emotion or violence.

In Ephesians 4:31 the apostle Paul details six different kinds of anger: bitterness, wrath, anger, clamor, slander and malice. Let's take a look at each of these briefly.

Bitterness: anger turned inward.
A bitter person focuses his or her emotional attention on a hurt or grievance and allows it to fester and putrefy sections of his or her life. It renders people hypersensitive, moody, critical, and negative.

Wrath: volcanic anger, spewing and destroying.
Some people in their immaturity just explode with anger, yelling, moving, threatening, cursing, and even swinging until their energy is gone. Their partners are then often willing to do whatever they want just so they don't have to experience that eruption again.

Anger: settled anger and opposition to another person.
This is typical: "I am angry at that person." It does not have the outburst of wrath but is usually more focused at a particular person and more intent on revenge or getting its own way. It is the form of anger that focuses dislike against one person. It often results in being

alert to any and all forms that cause that particular person to lose. It is unfortunate, but this often happens in a marriage followed by a divorce. Your marriage partner is now the one person whom you want to lose in every part of his or her life and in every situation.

Clamor: anger turned into yelling.

In the Ephesians 4:31 passage the word clamor is the Greek word *krauge*, which is a transliteration of the sound that a crow makes. It came to mean yelling, noisy, and irritating sounds. I remember one woman who learned to control her children and her husband by yelling at them. Even when she was talking at a low volume it had a yelling quality to it. They learned to be outside of yelling distance as much as possible.

Slander: anger turned into razor blades of truth and rumor used to cut one's reputation to pieces.

This may be the woman who endures her husband's destroying her expectations and dreams for a particular event but who then tells all of his dirty secrets to her friends. Or, it may be the husband who puts up with his wife's contrary point of view but then spends increasing amounts of time with his friends, running her down and making her look stupid. It's the form of anger that says, "I may not have the strength to challenge you directly, but I will make you pay."

Malice: anger turned into an evil scheme.

The person with malice allows his anger to become a plan to do his spouse harm. This may be how payback affairs take place, or it may be how a spouse is murdered. It might be how a marriage is destroyed financially or where a lawyer is encouraged to reveal details that will really damage a spouse in court. Malice moves beyond normal anger in that the normal boundaries of right and wrong are gone, and anything that will really hurt, wound, or destroy the other person is considered and acted upon.

Abusive Behavior

Abuse includes actions, words, and attitudes that oppress, afflict, harm, or denigrate a partner. There is a difference between accusations and abuse. Abuse seeks to diminish or oppress another person. Some men have resorted to physical or sexual violence against their wives to prove they are right or in charge. Some men and women feel they must emotionally pummel their spouse so they can remain in charge or dominate. There are a number of different kinds of abuse: verbal, emotional, physical, mental, and sexual. All of them are immature and show that one partner is unwilling to have an adult conversation on sensitive subjects. If one spouse is always wrong, then usually there is some form of abuse present. If one spouse is always apologizing but the other spouse never apologizes, it is a warning sign that abuse may be present. Men and women can abuse their partners until they feel the partner is always the reason for the problem. This is the position an abuser always wants his mate to be in. It is often the man who abuses his wife, but this is not the only form of abuse. It is usually the more aggressive and dominant personality that can become the abuser. The more passive or agreeable personality tries to make peace and is forced into apologizing.

Let me say a word to abusers. It does not matter whether you meant to harm anyone. It matters what you did to gain and keep control over that person. Mature people do not expect to win always. Mature people do not expect that everything will go their way. I have heard over and over again from abusers that they did not intend to harm, oppress, frighten, or devalue their mate. What matters is that they did. To gain or keep things going their way, abusers use every available means. If you force someone through the threat of violence to act a certain way, it is abuse. If you twist events and motives so the other person feels you are innocent and the victim is guilty, it is abuse. If you force someone into sexual relations against his or her will, it is abuse. If you hit, grab, or hurt your spouse physically, it is abuse. If you use your volatile rage to get a person to give in to your way of thinking, it is abuse. If your every word, suggestion, command, or idea must be obeyed, it is abuse.

Two adults in a marriage talk, discuss, learn, grow, negotiate, wait, and seek wisdom together. Do not be immature. No one person has all the wisdom all the time on the front end of a discussion. Yes, in the military, commands and even suggestions must be carried out without question, but a marriage is not a military organization. Yes, the husband has been charged biblically with the responsibility of being the head of the home, and that means he is responsible for making the wisest decision. He must choose to go against what he wants if it is not the wisest decision in a given situation.

Addiction

An immature reaction to pain or wounds by covering them up with some improvised "medication" may become an addition. The medication might be alcohol, drugs, food, videos, pornography, sex, or prescription drugs. The common denominator is the avoidance of dealing with some issue or hurt or wound by hiding from the difficulty through the so-called medication. It is immature because it doesn't deal with the real issue; it just masks it. Eventually the medication and your need for it will become a big problem. But that is not the real issue. The wounds in your life, the event you have never told anyone about, or the guilt you want to forget are the real issues. Bring them out in the open and be free of the power of the medication. In my years of marriage counseling, I have dealt with people's addiction to all kinds of things. It is always better when they find a safe person—a pastor, counselor, friend, or an authority figure—to begin dealing with the real issue, the wound or the guilt.

Apathy

Apathy is withdrawing from active participation in the marriage. It is a "Whatever" perspective. It is when a person says to himself or herself, "If this is the way it is going to be around here, I will not be emotionally invested here." More and more men and women are withdrawing from their marriages and home life as a silent protest that things are not the way they would like them to be. It is initially a strategy to get your own way, but it usually becomes a way of interacting in this arena of your life. People may be engaged and full of energy in other parts of their lives, but when they're home, they withdraw their full presence. This passive form of punishment is immature. You cannot build a great marriage unless you engage in discussion and involvement. Yes, there will be some areas where your ideas will not win, but that should not cause you to withdraw. It should cause you to engage with your partner even more, so you can build something unique together.

Adultery

The ultimate demonstration of selfishness and rebellion, other than murder, is adultery. It breaks the bonds of trust and commitment. Affairs never produce what they promise. They do not help the marriage or even the adulterer. They are selfish punishments, solutions, and distractions. One's life is never better because of an affair, nor are affairs ever a replacement for real discussion and involvement with one's spouse. Often an affair presents itself as a possibility exactly when difficult and crucial decisions need to be made in the marriage. If a husband or wife is willing to explore more thoroughly the way his or her spouse thinks or feels, there is room for significant relational growth. But an affair just seems easier than the work of really understanding oneself or one's mate.

Annoying Behavior

This is when people increase behaviors they know irritate or annoy their mate. It is a "polite" way of lodging your protest over a decision or direction. It usually isn't the end of the marital foolishness but the first step toward more significant immature behaviors. It is very childish and immature. Instead of talking about one's feelings and thoughts and looking for options and ways to incorporate new ideas into one's home and marriage, the person has resorted to being annoying and irritating.

Denial

Denial is deciding to stop meeting the needs of your spouse in some way as a protest. We most often hear about this as a wife making her husband sleep on the couch or saying she has a headache to avoid lovemaking. But men also act in these immature ways. "If my wife needs honor, then I will not give her a compliment no matter how beautiful she looks or how wonderful she is." "If my wife needs conversation, then I don't want to talk." "If my wife needs a date, then I am too busy to break away and do something like that." Whenever either a husband or a wife denies his or her mate what that other person needs to thrive in the marriage, it demonstrates immaturity. Everyone must realize that the overall health of the relationship is more important than lodging one's protest. You don't win anything by denying the other person what he orshe needs.

Demands

An injured or upset spouse may begin to make strong, even emotional, demands. The strength of the demands comes from the reaction to not getting his or her way in a previous discussion or argument. This immature technique is a form of an "eye for an eye and a tooth for a tooth." "Because you made me do _____, then I demand that you do _____." The answer, however, is not to deny or give in to the demands. The answer is to have a mature discussion about the issue that brought about the demands. Go back and start talking about the issue, and keep talking until everybody is comfortable with the decision that is made. If the decision needs to be unmade, then unmake it.

Dishonesty

Lying is often about spending, pornography, or some other guilty pleasure that soothes the difficulty of giving in to your mate. Lying is immature and lies will always unravel, so a solid marriage cannot be built upon lies. Married partners do not have to tell their spouses everything they have ever done or said, but solid marriages are built on truth, not lies. Many times people in a marriage think that if their partner does not find out about the lie, they are okay, but that is not true. Your partner is not your parent or your warden; your spouse is the person you need to trust to build a great life. Your partner needs to know what is really going through your mind and what your real desires involve. A number of couples have experienced a rebirth of their marriage (especially middle-aged couples) when they stopped pretending that they liked doing something and really became honest about what they would like to explore. That includes hobbies, travel, friends, churches, recreation, movies, etc.

Yes, some husbands and some wives are not interested in what their spouse really thinks or feels, and, of course, they will never really know until they find out. I recommend that you talk through your real feelings with a safe friend, counselor, pastor, or mentor to gain wisdom and to explore your ideas before presenting them to your spouse.

Depression

This is a phony, "You hurt my feelings. Poor me. I'm just a martyr. Pity me." Many women especially have learned that if they appear wounded, hurt, or on the verge of tears, their spouse will give them what they want. This often works because men do not know how to deal with their wives' emotions or negativity. The real answer is to have a rational discussion after the negative emotion is dissipated. A helpful interactive conversation cannot happen in the face of strong emotion. Some people have learned to control or punish their spouse through this put-on sadness. It is extremely immature and causes your spouse not to want to have a real conversation with you. It also causes your spouse to keep from making the right decisions, opting regularly instead for the emotionally safe decision.

I remember working with a woman who began to pout when things didn't go her way. Her husband was completely taken off-guard by that behavior. Eventually he learned that this was the way his wife's mother had controlled her father, so his wife was just act-ing out previous modeling. The husband learned to confront this behavior with a request for a grown-up conversation about what was bothering his wife. His wife eventually realized she did not need to act that way but could, instead, state her reasons and discuss her point of view with her husband without the emotional display.

Disrespect

When an immature person focuses on his or her spouse's weaknesses, flaws, and shortcomings, he or she is showing disrespect. Realize that everyone is a conglomeration of both good and bad actions, qualities, and attitudes. What many people do not see is that respect is not something that someone earns; it is something we give the other person. Respect is a mental perspective. Respect is a lens through which we can choose to see other people. Disrespect decides to focus on the negative, usually because someone hurt us or blocked us in some way. We often put on the glasses of disrespect in order to win a point in an argument or to comfort ourselves when we have lost an argument. If we keep the glasses of disrespect on very long, it will be highly destructive to our marriage. It is hard, if not impossible, to build a great marriage when there is little or no value placed on your spouse.

I remember one woman who focused her attention on her husband's shortcomings in an attempt to motivate him to do some of the things she wanted him to do around the house. Her constant "motivation" did not energize him to do what she wanted but instead motivated him to go fishing, spend time at work, and volunteer at the church. Unfortunately, she never learned that a man is drawn toward any place where he gets respect and admiration, and he avoids any place where he will be devalued.

Yes, it is not always easy to see the positive and the admirable, but it is there even if only in seed form. The more we avoid the glasses of disrespect and use the lenses of value, admiration, and encouragement, the better our marriage will become.

Destruction

Immature behavior that actually damages the other person in some way will result in destruction of the marriage. This kind of immaturity shows itself in various ways. It is designed to control and dominate the other person and must not be treated lightly. Many who resort to this behavior feel they do not have any other choice to be heard or to win. To fix this behavior we must show that there are other ways to interact and get one's point across. People who demonstrate this immaturity are often lose-lose negotiators. While they like to win, they are completely comfortable not winning, but they will make sure that you also do not win. They are not embarrassed or afraid of the negative consequences of their actions. In fact, in many cases they count on it. In their mind if the only way to keep their spouse from winning is to lose big, that is fine. The following are the most common destructive patterns in a marriage.

Physical: When one spouse actually physically harms the other person or his or her property.

Even if this involves only physical property, it is still serious. It means that the person is so frustrated that he or she feels the need to destroy something that is valuable to the spouse. If there is actual physical violence to the spouse, then the person has run out of ideas and needs significant help. Both the victim and the aggressor need individual help before such a marriage can be repaired. Usually, this kind of behavior calls for a time of separation before living together can be resumed. The victim must know how to stay out of a victim's mentality, and the aggressor must be able to demonstrate that he knows how to take alternative action when pressure is building. It is very serious. Unfortunately, we are seeing an increase in murder-suicide plans in which men especially do not know how to win, but they cause others to lose while they lose.

Financial: Immature behavior that is beyond just spending to salve a difficult period.

This is where people in their immaturity actually try to do damage to property, credit, or finances to exercise their will and make their partner pay attention to them. Filing for divorce, in some cases, is an example of this type of thinking. Some women feel they are out of options and do not know how to get their husbands to listen or back off, so they use the courts and the lawyers to wreak havoc on the finances so he will change or will just lose. I have seen a number of situations where women especially know that they will be thrown out of their house and be living in poverty with the children, but they need a way to strike back at their husband. Even though they know it will mean harm to the children, to themselves, and to their lifestyle, they push ahead because it will cause their husband to lose.

Threats/Fear: One spouse (often the man) threatens his spouse with her greatest fears so he can either control her or strike back at her for some perceived offense.

It could include threats to take the children or to harm them. It could be statements about revealing certain details about his wife's private life. It could be threats to release documents, photos, or video so she would lose her job or a promotion. (Of course, it could be the wife who makes such threats, including cutting off finances or conjugal visits.) The spouse does not know whether the threats are genuine, but she or he perceives them to be real.

If people have to resort to threats and fear to keep their marriage together or to have their point of view dominate, something is wrong. A marriage is a teamwork arrangement for the mutual benefit of both. Threats, fear, and control do not promote a healthy marriage. People who feel the need to threaten need to learn how to love at a new level to draw their spouse to them, and they need to understand how to have discussion without necessarily resolving things immediately.

Sexual: One spouse is sexually unfaithful to get back at the other spouse. Sometimes it is because the other partner has had an affair, but the core of this use of destructiveness is a desire to hurt, wound, or punish the spouse. This can extend even to high-risk sexual activity, which may result in diseases that can then be passed on to the spouse so he or she is punished even more. Remember, often these people are lose-lose negotiators. Their particular immature goal is not that they would win but just that their spouse would lose. Playing sexual Russian roulette to hurt your spouse is a deeply flawed strategy and suggests a need for new methods for communicating desires, goals, hopes, and dreams with one's spouse.

Reputation/Slander: When destructiveness is aimed at the reputation of the spouse.
This often starts out as a kind of parlor game where you tell friends an embarrassing secret about your spouse. It can then become a regular habit of getting back at your spouse for various slights and obstacles. You begin to describe your spouse's actions to yourself and others as stupid and moronic. Eventually, all you see about your partner is where he or she is acting differently than you would have acted or is simply looking silly. This immature behavior seems the least severe of the group of destructive behaviors, but it does destroy. It can destroy promotions, careers, and especially desires. When slanderous remarks about another person are shared, it changes one's perspective about

that person. Destroying the reputation of your spouse will destroy your marriage if it is not stopped immediately.

All forms of destructiveness must be avoided, and serious responses to discourage that kind of behavior must be put in place.

Distance/Divorce

This immature behavior deals with wounds, offenses, and difficulties through distance. The distance may be emotional, physical, mental, or spiritual, but distance is the key. When people act out in these immature ways, they do not want to interact, dialogue, negotiate, and engage; instead they react and want to remove the offending person in some way.

Emotional distance can easily and quickly grow into a loveless marriage in which both parties have no feelings for each other because of the decision of one partner to turn off his or her emotions over some slight, offense, or wound. An emotional divorce is not the answer. Instead learn how to fall back in love with each other and stop retreating when things don't go your way.

A mental divorce is a marriage in which both parties have their mental arenas of interest and growth, but they never talk about them together. They may exchange "business" information to keep the marriage, home, or children functional, but the conversation does not touch the soul of either one. Sometime in the past, one of the parties pulled an immature stunt and shut the other spouse out of what interested him or her the most. Since then there has been a growing mental distance between them. Sometimes this is exacerbated by one party's getting extra training or more schooling in a particular area and not including his or her spouse in those areas.

Spiritual distance is shutting your spouse out of your spiritual life. Sometimes it involves not participating with your spouse in his or her spiritual pursuits—allowing your spouse to become a separate person spiritually that you know nothing about. This can often happen when one partner becomes a Christian and starts changing, and the other partner doesn't want to change and does not want to understand what the other spouse is experiencing.

Physical distance is obviously where the couple are living separate lives either in different locations or in the same home. I remember one couple who were married more than ten years and had never spent a whole year living in the same home together. While it may start as an immature behavior to protest a wound or strike a blow, it moves the marriage to a business relationship. Often times the unintended consequence of these immature behaviors is a bland and loveless marriage. It was meant as punishment and a way of saying change, but it became a prison for both parties. Your marriage can be different even if you have been living out this level of immaturity.

The Consequences of Immature Behaviors

What happens when you continue to act in an immature way toward your spouse? You pull your marriage out of the zone of intimacy and put it into the zone of conflict and then, eventually, into withdrawal. What zone are you in right now? You must apologize for immature behaviors and engage in making a better marriage. If one or both of you keeps acting immaturely, you will kill your marriage as you back toward withdrawal and eventually some form of divorce. If you were to put an X to mark the zone that your marriage is in right now, where would it be?

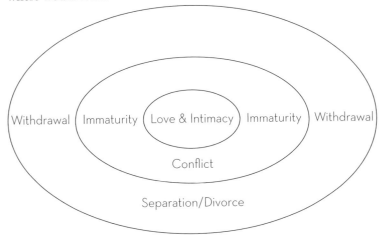

The Eight Solutions to Immature Behaviors

All of us tend to be immature at various times in our lives. It never helps our marriage. The question is whether or not you are ready to fix the damage you've done. It will take work. In some cases it will take a significant commitment of time and emotional energy, but there are solutions. There is hope.

Solution #1: Stop Acting in Immature Ways.

The first solution to the problem of immature behaviors is to stop acting in immature ways no matter what is happening around you. It would seem to go without saying that when you are being immature, you should stop. But it is important for me to say it: "Stop being immature!" It feels so right to protect yourself against your spouse's aggressiveness or immaturity, but acting immaturely for any reason does not help your marriage. When you find yourself being immature, stop and do something else or do nothing. Do not continue being immature. It does not matter why you are being immature. You must stop immediately and begin acting in a mature manner, or your marriage will not improve. Yes, I know that your stopping does not insure that your spouse will stop, but at least there will be one mature person in the marriage.

Over years of marriage counseling I have encountered men and women engaged in different levels and all kinds of immaturity from the silly to the deadly serious. One of the key first steps to fixing their marriages is to have them stop acting in those immature ways. It never fixes anything for a person to continue to yell or slander his or her spouse behind the spouse's back. It never helps the relationship if one person spends money the couple doesn't have or for one partner to seek comfort through an affair. All of the immature ways that have been listed in this section are counterproductive to a healthy marriage. In most cases people cannot see what the right thing to do is until they have stopped acting in immature ways. I believe that is why Jesus says that when a person is caught in adultery, he or she must cut out the offending relationship immediately, even if it is like losing a right hand or right eye (see Matt. 5:27-30). Immaturity brings a blindness that hides the wise course of action.

Take the Immature Behaviors Inventory at the end of this section. Admit which immature behaviors you have done and even the ones you are doing now. Find a way to stop. If it is easy to stop, then stop. If it takes a more detailed plan, start planning and acting in the right direction. If it requires seeing a counselor, pastor, or lawyer, then make the appointment. If no one knows what you are doing, bring it into the open with some safe people and figure out a way to stop. Obviously, seek God's face in prayer, but also start meditating on becoming mature in your marriage. Actually picture yourself acting in the way that would please Christ. If you can't picture yourself acting in a mature way (scriptural way), you will never be able to do it.

Do not be drawn into your spouse's immaturity. If your spouse knows how to push all your buttons, find a way to hide your buttons or de-emotionalize them. Many marriages stay in a constant state of confusion and dysfunction because everybody keeps being immature. One of you needs to start being mature. It might as well be you. One of the most exciting times in a marriage is when one person in the marriage refuses to play the game and gets off the merry-go-round of immaturity. The best chance to have a joyful marriage is to become a mature adult and invite your spouse to do the same. In the beginning most spouses do not believe your new level of control, and they may put on a bigger fuss because you are no longer fighting. Stay the course and continue to act in a mature way, whatever that looks like in the face of the particular immaturity of your spouse. Gently invite your spouse to join you in a mature relationship of joy and depth. It may take quite a while for your spouse to give up his or her immature ways.

Solution Number #2: Make Real Apologies.

The second solution to immature behaviors is to make a genuine apology to your spouse, restoring trust and the opportunity to love. We need to know how to formulate an apology for the times when we damage our relationships. Effective apologies are listed first because they are the most important and should be used regularly. If you are not apologizing on a regular basis, you probably aren't discerning the climate of your marriage.

An effective apology has six essential ingredients: being gentle in spirit, seeking education, admitting wrong, seeking forgiveness, describing a repentance plan, and testing for openness. An effectual apology allows your relationship to move past what happened and get back on track.

Be Gentle in Spirit.

Proverbs 15:1 says, "A gentle answer turns away wrath, But a harsh word stirs up strife." When a person is upset with you, be gentle and soft in your tone and mannerisms. It is amazing what takes place when you speak softly to someone who is irate. It is like a secret salve that calms them down. The rational person emerges to interact with what went wrong and how to repair it.

A person who is angry with you doesn't want to tell you what you did to hurt him. He wants you to figure it out for yourself. He wants to punish you. The only way to get him to open up to you is to approach him with quiet gentleness. You must assume it's your fault that he's upset and then be pleasantly surprised if it is someone or something else.

It's really important that you realize this is not "gentle in spirit" as defined by you. It is "gentle in spirit" as defined by *your spouse*. Jim was a hulking man about six-foot-three and 250 pounds. I remember his standing over his wife yelling, "I *am* being gentle!" It was like the force of his words blew her hair back. But in his mind he was being gentle. Everything about him said forceful, oppressive, and judgmental. I had to move him across the room. I had to make him sit down. I had to force him to whisper what he wanted to say. It took some time for Jim to grasp that gentle was defined by his wife, not by himself. He eventually understood. They worked it out, and their marriage was restored.

Seek Education.

Ask your spouse how you have hurt him (or her). This is really difficult because it requires humility. Here's an example: "I realize I have wounded and hurt you, and I'm sure I don't understand the extent of your hurt. Would you be willing to help me understand how I hurt you, so I don't do it anymore? I really want to learn, so please help me understand."

It may take a while before your spouse believes you're serious. It's important that you pay attention and really listen to what he or she says. Once your spouse gets going, you will have learned how to love him or her more effectively.

There will be times when you don't want to hear the answer. It may be trivial, inaccurate, or aggressive, but it is important you hear your partner out. Listen from your spouse's point of view rather than your own. There will be time later for clearing up misunderstand-ings. Don't try to correct the inaccuracies immediately; just listen. The solution could be that your spouse only needs you to hear his or her side of the story.

Great marriages allow both spouses to educate each other about what hurts them. The point here is to understand feelings and the reasons for those feelings.

Admit Wrong and Clear Up Misunderstanding.

It is best to admit you were wrong immediately. Get that out of the way. We naturally want to clear up misunderstandings and contextualize our mistakes first. That is all a part of face-saving and ego-defense mechanisms, which are perfectly understandable. But we need to go against our instinct in the repair of our marriage. When you have listened your spouse's concerns, complaints, or accusations, it is important first to admit your wrongs. There may be discussion on some things because you don't see them as errors or because they really are misunderstandings. But if you are willing to admit your guilt first, it allows your spouse to stop trying to get through your defenses. He or she will start working with you rather than remain-ing adversarial. Your spouse needs to hear you admit you were wrong so he or she can keep listening.

I have admitted I didn't say something in the proper way, even though I knew the content of the message was needed. I have admitted I could have handled a conversation better if my words weren't so blunt. I have admitted I was wrong to do one thing before something else, even though both needed to be done. Admit what you did wrong. Do not hold out with the thought that 98 percent of what you did was right. Do not resist admitting your guilt because you think it is trivial. Admit you were wrong when you were wrong, even if in your mind it was a minor issue.

Ask for Forgiveness.

It is important that the person who did the offense ask for forgiveness from the person he or she offended. It can be as simple as asking, "Will you forgive me?" and then waiting for a yes. It could involve a much more complex set of emotional responses that take time for the person to process. In such cases the offender may say, "I realize that for you to forgive me may take some time to think about, but I'm wondering if you could forgive me?" Sometimes the offended person will flippantly give an affirmative response too quickly. In those cases, the offender needs to repeat the question with a more gracious tone, "I appreciate your gracious response, but I know I have deeply hurt you. I really need to know if you are able to forgive me." This may be met by a pouring out of your sins, so the offended person can make sure you know what you did.

Discuss a Repentance Plan.

When an offense has been deep or repeated, there is often a need for a repentance plan. It will demonstrate that you have truly changed your mind about the offense and will no longer continue it. It resembles what we do with our children when we discipline them by asking, "What do you think we need to do, so you never do it again?" A repentance plan is important for serious offenses that need a demonstration of true contrition. It might be something like this, "I am truly sorry I wronged you in this way, and I never want to hurt you like that again. I know you have no way of knowing whether I really mean it, so let me say that if I do this again I will… (do the dishes for a week, wash your car, go to your favorite hobby) or you can… (spend a hundred dollars on a shopping spree, hide my golf clubs for a month, or order out for a whole week)." That kind of pre-arranged reminder is much better than making a spouse sleep on a couch, burning the toast, slamming the cupboards, or seething for three days.

Test for Openness.

After a real apology has been made and accepted, the offended person should be open to a renewed relationship. He or she may not be ready immediately to go to the depth of the relationship as before the offense, but there will be a renewed level of openness. Testing for openness demonstrates whether there has been a true reconciliation of the relationship. Many times people pretend to forgive but still hold you guilty for the things you did. A test of openness will reveal that.

To test for openness, evaluate how easily this person talks with you. Offer a hug and see if he or she hugs back. The hesitancy that was present before you asked for forgiveness should have disappeared.

Marriage Solutions and Exercises

- Write the six steps of a good apology on a card to carry with you.

- Make an apology to your spouse for one thing in the past.

- What does your spouse think you need to apologize for? Ask him or her.

- Really listen to his or her perspective instead of defending your position.

- Don't automatically apologize for everything you've ever done. Your spouse may not be able to handle knowing everything you've done. Some things you have done are for you and God to deal with privately. The key ingredient in this issue is a willingness to admit your mistakes.

Solution #3: Have Alignment Conversations.

The third solution for immature behaviors is to learn how to have regular alignment conversations. We all have expectations for our marriage and our spouse. It is best to clarify them before an event so that both can see each other's expectations. The first kind of alignment conversation would be in advance of a potentially difficult situation. Ask your spouse to sit down with you and clarify expectations.

- "Let's take a look at this weekend and align our expectations as to how we're spending our time and who will do what and when."

- "Can we talk about how you see this weekend and how I see this weekend so that we're on the same page?"

Much of our difficulty with each other is because of unclear and unmet expectations. One person saw the weekend one way and the other saw it differently. Unless you talk about it before the weekend, there may be an argument.

The second kind of alignment conversation takes place after a fight or argument.

- "Honey, I need to talk with you about what was going on in my mind when we had those tense moments the other day."

- "I was expecting you to ____. When that didn't happen, I got upset and couldn't control my emotions."

When a fight or argument is discussed calmly and thoughtfully regarding the expectations that started it, great progress is possible. Anger is the result of unmet or unrealistic expectations, so getting to the bottom of why the flare-up took place is very helpful. You may be surprised at the reasons you are fighting.

A third kind of alignment conversation is communicating your relational needs.

- "At this point in my life, I find that I need more from you in this area than I have needed before."

- "It may be because of the present situation, but I feel like I am starved for _____. Can you focus more in this area, please?"

- "I sense that something is different between us. I would like to clarify how to best meet your needs rather than guess what would make you happy."

As you continue to be together, you will need different things in different ways to love each other. It is better to have open discussions about what you need rather than hope the other person will guess correctly. Your spouse is most likely not going to guess accurately because he or she mpletely different person from you. We'll go into more detail on this subject in the next chapter. Rather than hide the fact that a particular need is not being met in your marriage, have a good conversation about it. That is healthy and mature.

Marriage Solutions and Exercises

- Have an alignment conversation with your spouse about the coming weekend.

- What are you expecting to happen this next week? Discuss it with your spouse.

- Ask, "If we were to do _____ your way, how would you see it taking place?"

- Have an alignment conversation about your last fight. Arguments and fights happen because of unrealistic expectations, so get them out in the open and talk about them rationally.

- "Here is what I was expecting right before we got into it."

- Go back and clarify expectations that caused an argument.

- Do not disagree with his or her expectations. Let your spouse express them.

Solution #4: Thoughtful Requests

The fourth solution to the problem of immature behaviors is to make thoughtful calm requests about what you need rather than emotional demands or cryptic hidden messages. Joel asked if he could talk with me after a session I had led at a men's retreat. Joel was disturbed that his wife never seemed to reciprocate the love he gave her. According to him, she had acknowledged that he loved her more fully than she was able to love him back. He had been waiting a year for her to begin meeting his needs, but it never happened. I told Joel that since a woman's needs are totally different from a man's, sometimes the other person needs to hear direct, but gentle, statements about what you need him or her to do. I suggested Joel sit down with his wife, Jennifer, and emphasize his love for her and write down three to five specific needs he was hoping she could meet at a new level. That kind of nonjudgmental clarity and encouragement to love at a new level works well.

Too often we expect our spouse to read our mind about what we need or to correctly decipher the coded message that we send. Instead of doing what comes naturally, be lovingly clear. In many cases the only time a spouse is clear is in the midst of a fight, and the message is ignored because of the emotions wrapped around it. Start making thoughtful requests of your spouse. Sit with your spouse in a place where you won't be disturbed and talk about the months ahead. Make sure you both have a calm demeanor and that you have at least 30 minutes to chat. You might say something like:

- "Honey, I love you, and I deeply enjoy being married to you. I'm not completely sure of the reasons, but I need some things from you at a level I haven't needed before."

- "I have been reading _____ or listening to _____, and I realize I need more honor (or respect, intimacy, companionship, understanding) from you."

- "What we have right now is great. However, with the things I am facing this next year, I will need more _____ ____ from you to help me through it."

- "I am facing difficulty right now, and I need you to walk with me through it at a deeper level than before. I also realize that you are going through your own challenges, and I want to explore new ways to meet your needs."

Similar conversations between my wife and me have been so helpful that we have incorporated them into our weekly staff meeting. These meetings are a chance to talk about issues without making them a big deal. We go through the ten relationships of life and discuss what needs to be planned, done, changed, and improved to make each of these relationships more abundant. If you can learn to have a calm and thoughtful conversation about what you both need, it is amazing how quickly things can improve. I have regularly heard others say, "Is that all you want?"

Marriage Solutions and Exercises

- Ask your spouse about areas that may be limiting you. Be careful this discussion is not just an opportunity to unload. We have the capacity to make only one significant change every six months to a year.

- Ask your spouse what five simple things you could do to make you the ideal spouse. Ask him or her to actually say or write the response.

Solution #5: Add More Love.

The fifth solution to the problem of immature behaviors is to add more love to cover over the immaturity. In my mind, Ann is a legend. Her husband was involved in an affair. This timid woman decided that the way to save her husband and her marriage was to love him so thoroughly that he would have no reasonable choice but to come back to her and the kids. He had been seduced into a wild party life by a woman he met at a local gym. Ann began competing for her husband's attention. She "upped her game" as she described it. He noticed immediately. She also confronted his paramour and let his boss know what was going on. His boss, while not wanting to get involved, was still willing to help Ann love her husband at new levels. It took lots of prayer, asking people to confront her husband, really understanding what made him tick, and loving him more completely than he had ever been loved before; but she did win her husband back to the marriage. She won even though lots of people were telling her that he was not worth it and that he did not deserve all of her efforts. They were right, but Ann loved him anyway. It took three or four months for the power of her love to work its magic, but her husband came back and was completely chastised by her overwhelming love.

I do not always recommend what Ann did for spouses who are being so openly selfish, but it was clearly what God was directing her to do, and it worked. Remember there are eight biblical solutions to SAD behaviors, not just one.

One of the key solutions to SAD behaviors is to add more love to your relationship. The magic ointment of all great marriages is maximum amounts of love (meeting needs, pursuing, pleasing). Some couples instinctively assume the way to get a spouse's attention is to withhold something important. Usually that is followed by an emotional response about how things have to change. This withholding strategy will not work long-term because the deprived party resents the message. Withholding what he or she needs takes away the energy to make your marriage work. If you want to improve your marriage, increase your love and make thoughtful requests for your spouse to do the same. When your spouse is receiving more love from you, he or she will be motivated to reciprocate.

Ann did what Jesus tells us to do when someone offends us or has become our enemy. He says that we will be tempted to follow the dictum, "An eye for an eye and a tooth for a tooth" (Matt. 5:38). Instead, Jesus says to "Love your enemies, bless those who curse you, do good to those who hate you, and pray for those who spitefully use you and persecute you" (NKJV). When we are facing someone who is being selfish or demanding or destructive, love him or her more, not less. Overcome their evil (selfishness) with good. Selfishness is usually an attempt to meet a felt need. Loving the person more means finding those needs and meeting them so the other person can settle down to a less needy position. Many times what is prompting the selfish and foolish behavior is that there is just not enough love flowing in the marriage. Sometimes more love can divert the other person from the foolish and destructive things that he or she is doing.

On numerous occasions I have found myself wanting to set the record straight or straighten out my wife, but each time I felt God prompting me to love her more instead. That was always the right idea even though I didn't want to act that way. Meeting my wife's relational needs more fervently caused difficulties to melt away as she responded in-kind. I believe when a husband or wife truly is meeting the needs of his or her spouse, thoughtful, practical requests meet with virtually no resistance.

Marriage Solutions and Exercises

- Ask the question, "How can I love my spouse more?" and "What more can I do to fill him or her emotionally, spiritually, relationally, and mentally?" After you have loved your spouse with renewed commitment, you have the leverage to ask that your needs be met at a new level.

- Focus your time, energy, and resources on meeting your spouse's relational need that will have the greatest impact.

- Have a conversation with your spouse about his or her needs. What does he or she need to be able to think of you as the perfect or ideal spouse? More handholding, more sex, more romantic walks or dates, more admiration, less sarcasm, more involvement at home?

Solution #6: Change an Immature Behavior.

The sixth solution for immature behavior is to aim at change and not stop until you get it. There are some behaviors that must change, or the marriage cannot survive. Whether you are the offending or the offended spouse, those behaviors must change. The behavior cannot be ignored. Here are a few toxic and destructive behaviors:

- Affairs
- Alcoholism
- Drug abuse
- Gambling addiction
- Violence against your spouse
- Criminal behavior
- Absenteeism
- Imprisonment or denial of freedom
- Disloyalty
- Tax evasion
- Unwillingness to work
- Verbal and/or emotional abuse

Those behaviors will ultimately destroy a marriage. As stated in the previous material on dealing with level three immature behaviors, these actions are truly toxic and must be removed before significant healing to the marriage can take place. When those kinds of personally destructive behaviors take place, it is important to realize that in every marriage there are three clients: the husband, the wife, and the marriage. Until the offending spouse is willing to deal with the highly destructive behavior, the marriage will not make much progress, and a line in the sand may need to be drawn.

Changing these kinds of issues requires specific knowledge, expert help, and a long-term plan. It took a long time to spiral down into these actions, and it will most likely (unless God does a huge miracle) take a long time to walk out into freedom. It is more like Joshua's battle to conquer the land than the parting of the Red Sea. Both are miracles, but one is immediate, and the other is progressive. There are counselors, seminars, and recovery groups in every major city that deal with the particular pathology of these destructive behaviors. Learn, grow, confront, stop denying, stop enabling, process the pain, and face the guilt. Realize that if you keep doing what you have always done, you will always get what you have always been getting. If you are after different results, you need to change something. Make sure you have studied enough and gotten good counsel to know what to change first and what to change next. Changing severe immature behaviors requires sustained change; but the love, harmony, and acceptance you crave can be rebuilt.

I have watched wives who have learned how to deal with their alcoholic husbands and help them hit bottom so they repent and seek God and then are able to rebuild their families. I have seen husbands who have worked through their wife's affair and even loved the children that came from their wives' illegitimate actions. It took hard conversations, repentance, new levels of accountability, and new levels of love and honesty, but it started with mature action on one person's part that was not going to let the immaturity of the other destroy the marriage. Changing immature behaviors, especially those that are the most damaging, is not easy; but they will destroy the marriage if you don't try. You might as well learn how to bring about positive change rather than let those behaviors destroy the marriage.

It will most likely require the help of a support network to bring about changes needed to stop dumping destructive toxins into your marriage. Take the action and get started. Your marriage is worth fighting for!

Marriage Solutions and Exercises

- Honestly answer the following questions:
  - o Do others think you are damaging your marriage?
  - o Are there any immature behaviors that need to be changed?
  - o Is your spouse doing anything that is damaging your marriage?
  - o If others knew the truth, would they think you need to change?

- If your partner is involved in a damaging behavior, ask yourself, "What can I do that will stop my partner's immature behavior?"

- Contact someone today. But beware; too often what seems like help merely enables the destructive behavior.

The following table can expose those immature behaviors that are in the way of a great marriage. Be careful about who sees what you have written here. I have given you a small place to write, but it will probably be better to write on a separate piece of paper in a journal or protected place.

My spouse wants me to limit the following actions, words, activities, and/or relationships for the sake of our marriage:	
I need to limit or eliminate the following actions, words, activities, and/or relationships to improve my marriage:	

I need to talk with my spouse about limiting his or her involvement in the following actions, words, activities, and relationships for the sake of our marriage:	
I absolutely will not stop the following actions, words, activities, and/or relationships:	

Solution # 7: Confrontational/Clarifying Conversation

The seventh way of solving immature behaviors in a marriage is to have a clear conversation. It is amazing how many people shy away from helpful conversations. If a marriage is going to work, there needs to be direct communication about the good, the bad, and the irritating. Most people were never trained how to interact clearly about what irritates them. Without a way to express those crucial feelings, we explode onto the other person, spewing pent-up anger. The only time real honesty is communicated is in the midst of a fight, but then it is wrapped in so much negative and critical emotion that the content of the message is lost. The problem is that we choose to talk about the bad stuff at exactly the wrong time. Our spouse can't hear what we're saying because our emotional outburst drowns out the message. Usually, a retaliatory response rears up to defend good intentions, and the message is lost.

A good marriage has plenty of conversations about what the two parties need to make their marriage work. Have clarifying conversations when everyone is calm—before an event, not during or after. Unstable couples tend to explode or give each other the silent treatment rather than communicate what they are expecting. I have found that speaking truth calmly and rationally is essential. Here are a few ways to get the point across:

- "Honey, I love you, and I think you are terrific. But when you do _____, it hurts my feelings."
- "I know that this may not be a big deal to you, but it is to me."
- "I don't know whether you realize that when you _____, it makes me feel _____,, and I find myself having a hard time responding to you."

There may be many SAD behaviors to address with your spouse, but you should talk about only three to five over the course of the next two years. Be sure you choose those that will make the most difference. You'll have to let go of the others for now. Focus on the majors and forget the rest.

I realize it may be intimidating to have a serious conversation about something that really bothers you, but if you have loved your spouse by meeting his or her needs, this conversation can take place. If you have not been meeting your spouse's relational needs, the conversation should wait.

Marriage Solutions and Exercises

- Ask your spouse if you can clarify some things in order to strengthen your marriage. Realize he or she probably doesn't realize what bothers you.

- Tell your spouse precisely what the issue is and what you prefer he or she do instead. It is not enough to point out a problem—suggest an alternative behavior as well.

- The ground rule is that there must be enough love (meeting needs) already going on to handle this type of discussion.

- Allow time and emotional space for your spouse to disagree with your assessment and alternative behavior. Listen, take notes, and let him or her vent.

- Do not allow your spouse to switch the subject to your faults. Respond with, "Yes, there are a number of areas that I can improve, but right now we are talking about one specific behavior adjustment I would like you to make."

Solution # 8: Patience and a Change of Focus

The eighth solution to immature behaviors is to adopt a long-term patience with your spouse and his or her needed changes. Many times we get out of sync with our mates because we focus on weaknesses and mistakes rather than strengths. If your focus stays negative, you won't be able to develop a good marriage. Each partner in the marriage must choose to be optimistic about what God will do in the future. Hope is essential for building a good marriage. Of course marriages have areas that need improvement, but try to focus on positive qualities. I have found a marriage will improve significantly with a healthy dose of patience, followed by a new focus on your spouse's strengths. If he or she changes, it won't be because of your harping. It will be because your spouse wants to please you because you've been so supportive.

There are times to keep silent, praying your partner will see and correct a selfish behavior (That does not include lethal or dangerous behaviors.). The point of this solution is to start focusing on the strengths of the other person instead of believing that your life is doomed until your partner changes to please you. Become your mate's strongest advocate and convince yourself that the strengths outweigh the negatives. It will mean you may have to distance yourself from friends and/or relatives who constantly focus on what your spouse is doing wrong. There will come a time when your spouse is ready to deal with whatever drives you nuts right now, but it won't happen as long as you are constantly harping about it. Your spouse needs to feel you're on his or her side unconditionally, even if that area doesn't change. As weird as it sounds, this is usually when the other person finds the energy and ability to change. Do not let what annoys you about your spouse be your focus. Force your mind to rehearse his or her good points.

Marriage Solutions and Exercises

- Choose which of your mate's behaviors you are willing to leave to God to change.

- Pray honestly and fervently about those behaviors.

- Make a long list of your spouse's strengths. A person makes the greatest changes in the areas of strengths, not weakness. It is, therefore, beneficial to help your spouse become stronger in his or her strengths. It can help to see a major weakness as a part of a strength misapplied or something holding back a strength.
- Do not make a list of your spouse's weaknesses. Focus on his or her strengths.

Solutions	Explanation
Stop Acting in Immature Ways	Whenever an immature behavior is discovered it is stopped immediately. Do not act in this way any longer.
Make Real Apologies	Understand your spouse's point of view and admit you were wrong if you were.
Have Alignment Conversations	Interact ahead of time about what you expect to have happen so there are no surprises or disappointments.
Thoughtful Requests	Gently and thoughtfully ask for what you need from your spouse rather than ranting or pouting.
Add More Love	Meet your spouse's needs at a new level to smooth over the difficulties and provide the desire for him or her to reciprocate.
Change an Immature Behavior	Admit that you are doing something that is damaging your marriage, and do what it takes to change that behavior. Realize that your spouse is continuing in an immature behavior that needs to change no matter the cost.

Confrontational/ Clarifying Conversation	Seek clarification about an event or behavior that you saw or heard about. If it is appropriate, make it clear to your spouse that what he or she is doing is not acceptable and that change or progress is needed in that area.
Patience and a Change of Focus	Focus on progress in a few areas and give lots of time and room for improvement in other areas. Be patient with all except the huge issues.

Immature Behaviors Inventory

Which of the immature behaviors have you engaged in?

If we were to ask your spouse, which immature behaviors would he or she say you tend to use?

Which three do you use the most?

Which ones does your spouse tend to use?

Immature Behavior	Spouse	Self
Sarcasm/Slander		
Silence		
Spending		
Sick/Sleep		
Stupid/Irrational		
Selfish		
Accusations/Blame		
Anger		
Abusive Behavior		
Addiction		

Apathy		
Adultery		
Annoying Behavior		
Denial		
Demands		
Dishonesty		
Depression		
Disrespect		
Destruction		
Distance/Divorce		

Summary of the Problem of Immature Behaviors

We are all selfish and immature at times. We think about our comfort, what we want, and how we prefer life to be. A good marriage brings two people together who lay aside their selfishness and put the other person first. The team must win before the individual wins. Marriages disintegrate when one or both partners go after selfish wins at the expense of the team win. There will always be things that you would like, but they may require a loss for your spouse. Those wins must be left unclaimed. That may be hard, but it is how great marriages are built.

When selfishness and immaturity take over in your relationship, you will inevitably have conflict. Your spouse will hopefully make allowances for momentary lapses and take action that will bring you back to team play. Be mature even when you don't want to be. Remember that there are eight general solutions to SAD behaviors. Work on these solutions to keep your marriage enjoyable and positive. Some couples have found it helpful to memorize this list or carry it around with them, so they are ready for the difficulties of marriage.

The Five Problems of Marriage

Ignoring Needs	Immature Behaviors	Clashing Temperaments	Competing Relationships	Past Baggage
Wife's Needs Honor Understanding Security Building Unity Agreement Nurture Defender **Husband's Needs** Respect Adaptation Domestic Leadership Intimacy Companionship Attractive Soul and Body Listener	**Level 1** Thoughtless Immaturity **Level 2** Directed Immaturity **Level 3** Destructive, and/or Addictive Immaturity **Eight Solutions** Stop Further Immaturity Apology Alignment Thoughtful Requests More Love Change Behavior Clarify Patience			

Problem #3

Clashing Temperaments

Problem #3

Clashing Temperaments

Ps. 139:13-16; Phil. 2:1-4; Prov. 30:10-14

Overview

"Irreconcilable differences" was listed on the divorce papers. John and Sandy were just too different. They were opposites in almost every way. He was thoughtful, quiet, and predictable. She was loud, powerful, and craved adventure. It was so wonderful and exciting during dating, but then it slowly became intolerable. Another marriage was on the fast track to destruction. It didn't need to be that way. They had been a complement to each other in the early months and years of their marriage, but then each person retreated more and more into his own patterns and ways of living. What the spouse did and wanted to do made less and less sense. Eventually, it was just a business relationship with no joy and little conversation.

At one point, Sandy realized she did not want to live like this and left on a vacation with a friend. It was wonderful, exciting, and everything that she felt was missing in her marriage. She needed to be free from John, so she could live the life she deserved. She planned to leave her marriage because she and John were just too different. In her mind, she was still full of life, and he was just too boring. John was the anchor holding back the life she really wanted.

We all are different people, and we are naturally attracted to people who are different from us. Those differences are very attractive during the initial stages of a relationship, but then they begin to grate, repel, and need changing eventually.

I have watched this scenario play out over and over again with different couples. Sometimes it is the wife who needs to get away. Sometimes it is the husband who wants some "excitement" in his life. If the one who wants to get away actually acts on his or her plans, he or she usually goes through three to six years of bars, parties, relationships, and even marriages and then begins to appreciate the unique characteristics, temperament, and abilities of the first partner. He or she has chased after pleasure only to find it is not as satisfying as stability, family, commitment, and acceptance. If a couple can take a new look at themselves and their partner, they can inject fun, enjoyment, and effectiveness into their lives without getting divorced. When a couple embraces who they are and who their spouse is and then works hard to let their individual strengths make a great team, everybody wins.

God watched over our birth and made sure that we had the specific skills, temperament, abilities, gender, and sensitivities that He wanted (Ps. 139:13-16). That is true for every person, and we need to be accepted and appreciated for all the unique characteristics God wove into us. Our marriage is supposed to be one of the key places where we will always be applauded for our strengths and protected in the areas of our weaknesses. When we are attacked in our marriage for what we lack and hated for what we do well, the place of safety and love becomes a house of horrors and a place to avoid.

I have had couples pull back from the precipice of divorce and learn how to thrive by embracing their strengths and unique combinations. I have had others who had to follow their heart and, consequently, destroyed their families, their bodies, and their finances only to confess to me later that it was all a mistake, and they wish they could go back. Unless your spouse is doing immoral or illegal things, it is much better to work on the marriage than to go chasing a fantasy life that does not exist and cannot last.

What they both needed was to be accepted and enjoyed for who they were instead of measured against the other person's temperament, impulses, and style. Over the years, I have accumulated various ways of looking at the unique aspects of people. These tools help people get a clear picture of themselves and their mates. I use a number of assessment tools because no one test can give a complete picture of the multifaceted aspects of a person. Remember, no one assessment can explain anyone. We are complex beings made in the image of God with all types of mental, emotional, spiritual, and physical attributes that make us unique. Each of these assessments offers a snapshot of one small part of who a person really is. It becomes much easier to accept and appreciate your spouse when you realize that he or she is acting a certain way because of how God wired him or her. Your spouse is not doing something just because he or she knows it bugs you.

The Third Element in Marital Intelligence

Spousal differences illustrate the third major component in Marital Intelligence, Clashing Temperaments. Temperament is the consistent tendencies, patterns, reactions, and internal impulses that are a part of one's normal actions and responses to life. It is these internal temperament factors that define a large part of who we are and what we are like.

As most married couples find out, opposites attract until they are married and then they repel. Qualities that were initially attractive can become a source of irritation and difficulty. Wisdom suggests we accept our mate with his or her strengths, weaknesses, impulses, and orientations.

A complete acceptance of the core person provides a deep joy and strength. I have told couples I could not fix their marriage until they are willing to admit their spouse is different and celebrate the differences. The differences make it crucial to look at temperament if you want to approach marriage intelligently.

It is best to try to understand your mate from a number of different temperament parameters rather than just one assessment tool. In this chapter, we give a quick overview of four temperament assessment tools. Each one assesses different aspects of a personality and, when taken together, they show a more complete picture. I have found the following basic temperament assessment perspectives to be predictive for personal behaviors:

- Male and Female Characteristics
- Myers-Briggs Four Different Scales
- Four Ancient Personality Profiles
- Love Languages

Other helpful assessment tools I have used include Spiritual Gift Testing, Memory Eye Patterns, Life Experience Mapping, Natural Abilities Test, and Family Patterns & Events. Each temperament assessment tool has its strengths and weaknesses. The goal of these tests is to help you understand and accept the person you married. I am always encouraged when people realize their spouse is not wrong, just different. It is only in the understanding of differences that the wonder of marriage begins to unfold.

Let me give you an illustration of how temperament impulses make us different. In our kitchen there are several different appliances. We have a toaster, an electric can opener, a phone, a microwave, and a clock. Each one has gears, motors, and uses electricity, but what happens when we turn them on is completely different. It would be stupid to yell at the clock for not cooking the food. It would be ridiculous to talk to the toaster and expect other people to hear you. It would be counterproductive to carry a seething anger at the can opener for its inability to toast bread. It is the same with people. We all breathe air, have the same internal organs, walk, talk, and have a brain. But when each of us uses all of those things that God gave us, we do different things. Some build cabinets; some make speeches; some build organizations; some offer mercy; some cook. Each of us has been wired by God to make a unique contribution in this world and in our marriage. When the electricity of life is turned on, we do what we do. It is so much easier to let our spouses be who they are than to try to force a can opener to toast bread. I have watched people yell, scream, and carry seething anger at their spouse for being unable to do something they were never wired to do. That is idiotic. Now there are role expectations in every part of life, but the more the God-given wiring is allowed to express itself, the more everyone benefits. Wouldn't it be great if our spouse let us be who we are and then appreciated us for it? My kitchen is in harmony because I let the toaster toast, the phone take my calls, the can opener open my cans, and the microwave cook my snacks.

Let me give you a personal illustration. I am a lousy handyman. If I try to repair something, it will usually cost twice as much when we call the expert to fix it later. I am pretty good at giving speeches and writing books. My gracious wife has adapted to the fact that I am a disaster with tools, and she simply calls a handyman service to repair household items. She doesn't boil with rage at the fact that I can't repair anything. In fact, she ignores this area of nonstrength for me and praises me for my speeches and book writing. She accepts me as I am and then applauds me when I do what God wired me to do. That is how a great marriage should work.

It is instructive to notice the impulses, natural patterns, preferences, and orientations of both people in a marriage. Understanding the "wiring" of the individuals in the marriage can explain much about them. The "aha" moments are astounding when couples begin to understand each another.

Let me add that God has given each of us ten relationships with which to make a full life. Many couples in our modern era ask too much of their mates. They want their mates to totally fill up every part of their being. This is unrealistic. It is the whole of our lives that will fill up the whole of our being. We need a dynamic relationship with God, a fully developed soul, an engaging family, interesting and challenging work, a thriving church, a peaceful community, and enjoyable friends. All of these together touch and minister to the whole of our person.

Marital Intelligence Test

This test probes the actions necessary to have a great marriage. Do not be surprised by the results. Celebrate your strengths and work on improving your weak areas. Your spouse might respond differently to the same questions. The areas of differences are opportunities to grow and improve your marriage. Hopefully, this test will whet your appetite for the solutions in this book.

Problem #3
0 = Never; 1 = Rarely; 2 = Occasionally; 3 = Sometimes; 4 = Usually; 5 = Always

I accept my spouse the way he/she is without trying to change him/her.	0 1 2 3 4 5
I understand how my spouse's gender makes him/her different.	0 1 2 3 4 5
I know my spouse's dominant love languages.	0 1 2 3 4 5
I know how to speak my spouse's dominant love language.	0 1 2 3 4 5
I know whether my spouse is an extrovert or an introvert and how to value that and allow for it.	0 1 2 3 4 5
I know whether my spouse is an abstract thinker or a concrete thinker and how to value that and allow for it.	0 1 2 3 4 5
I realize how my spouse prefers to make decisions either objectively or personally and make allowances for that preference whenever possible.	0 1 2 3 4 5
I make room for my spouse's need for closure or spontaneity.	0 1 2 3 4 5
I understand my spouse's inner impulse for attention, control, peace, or perfection and do not demand that he/she change.	0 1 2 3 4 5
I feel accepted, not belittled or ignored by my spouse.	0 1 2 3 4 5
My unique point of view as a man or woman is valued and encouraged by my spouse.	0 1 2 3 4 5
My spouse knows my dominant love languages.	0 1 2 3 4 5
My spouse speaks love to me in my love language.	0 1 2 3 4 5
My spouse respects my extroversion or introversion and does not demand that I be something I'm not.	0 1 2 3 4 5
My spouse allows me to use my thinking style (abstract or concrete) without demanding that I be different.	0 1 2 3 4 5

My spouse and I understand and use my preference for objective or personal decisions to enhance our decisions and marriage.	0 1 2 3 4 5
If possible, my spouse allows me to bring closure to a situation or delay decisions, so I am comfortable.	0 1 2 3 4 5
My spouse knows my strongest internal impulse (attention, control, peace, or perfection) and, whenever possible, lets me be me.	0 1 2 3 4 5
Subtotal Section #3	

Add up your total. How did you do? Remember that these results reflect the current condition of your relationship. Realize, too, that no one is the perfect spouse. The two of you are completely different people. Those differences are what make a marriage wonderful. Two very different people can get along and thrive, but they must work at it. The solutions in this book *will* work.

The positive statements on the test outline a high standard of how we should treat one another. Start applying those truths, and your relationship will improve right away.

Scoring:

90 - 68: You have a very good marriage in this area. Keep it up. Keep digging to understand each other's internal impulses and basic wiring patterns. *Viva la difference!*

67 - 45: You have a good marriage that could be significantly improved by making more allowances for the differences in your temperaments. Pick one area in your spouse that you will make allowance for rather than seeing it as a moral issue.

44 – 22: There are some serious deficiencies in the expression of love in your marriage. Both partners are being damaged by the lack of room to be yourselves. You need to start working together, recognizing each other's temperament impulses as a plus rather than a minus. Start being a team. God put you together for a reason. A good marriage is not an absence of conflict but an abundance of love.

21 - O: There is a lack of acceptance and a significant amount of "my way is best" in your marriage. It takes only one person in the marriage to make a difference in the beginning. Schedule a meeting with a counselor or pastor. At least one of you needs to start studying the ways that you are different and how that drives the fights and loneliness you both feel.

Male and Female Characteristics

Let's start our examination of temperament characteristics with the most definitive and objective of the temperament measures: the basic differences between males and females. Some might argue that they are not temperament differences, but I would counter that maleness and femaleness involve internal "wiring" structures with internal impulses. God wired men and women differently, and it is very helpful to recognize the differences. Recent research suggests that there is more going on than what was previously thought.

Leonard Sax, in his fascinating book *Why Gender Matters,* cites numerous studies of actual physical and physiological differences between men and women. These gender differences should be understood and taken into account, especially in the marriage relationship. Let's take a look at seven of these differences.

Hearing

Numerous studies have shown conclusively that females hear 7 to 20 times better than males.[1] That difference may explain why many women think their husbands are yelling, and the men are shocked by that characterization. It also may explain why a husband often cannot hear his wife or does not fully understand what she is saying when she speaks in a normal tone to him. He is not ignoring her, nor is he not interested in paying attention.

Facial Expression

Another significant difference between men and women is their ability to recognize facial expressions accurately. Sax notes, "Most girls and women interpret facial expression better than most boys and men can."[2] That is what internally directs women to be face-to-face communicators. They pick up much more information from the nonverbal facial expressions than most men.

Researchers have found that women are more drawn to the fine detail of facial expression because they have more of a particular type of light receptor in their eyes that receives fine details. Men, on the other hand, have a much higher percentage of a different light receptor that notices motion and specific colors.[3] These differences in eye structure show up in the natural orientation of men and women. A man, in many instances, does not notice the nonverbal clues that his wife is convinced he is ignoring. Her eye is built to look straight at another person. Conversely, a man is built to be fascinated by larger movements and is thereby drawn to action.[4]

A practical consequence of this factor in my marriage is that when my wife needs to talk, I sit down across from her and focus all my attention on her face and what she is saying. That shows her that I love her and am listening with the proper level of interest. When I need to talk, my wife and I walk around the park or go for a drive. That allows us to focus our eyes on something moving in front of us rather than reading every reaction in her or my face. I find it easier to talk that way.

Language and Emotion

Another area of fascinating difference between males and females is in the ability to process and interact with emotions. Men and women feel and process emotions in different regions of the brain. Women and girls process emotion in the same place as their verbal centers and, therefore, are able to understand their feelings and put them into words quite easily. Men and boys, on the other hand, process emotions deep in the brain with little or no access to verbal expression. In other words, a young man may feel emotion, but he is not as sensitive to the emotion and is not able to verbalize it at all.[5]

Men and boys are not strongly connected to their emotions, as only a few neural pathways connect their emotional center to the verbal area of the brain. It is not that a man does not have all the emotions of his wife; it is that he is insensitive to that area of his life, and he has little ability to verbalize those emotions. Many wives have accused their husband of not wanting to share what they are feeling. It is true in a different way than she suspects. He is not in touch with the feelings that he is having, and he has no words to describe them. For a man, feelings are often only bombastic with emotions like love, hate, anger, etc.

On the other hand, women are fascinated by emotions, are able to differentiate all types of emotions, and have great facility in describing them. The question, "What are you feeling?" is a different question from, "What are you thinking?" for a woman. It is the same question for most men.

Geometry and Navigation

Another fascinating difference between men and women is that men and women use different parts of the brain for navigation, geometry, and math in general.[6] Sax notes that a woman's sense of direction and navigation is centered in her cerebral cortex, which is also the verbal center. That may be the reason she has an easier time asking and receiving directions verbally. In contrast, a man processes directions and navigation in the hippocampus, which is largely a nonverbal center of the brain. His mind is looking for nonverbal, absolute information that can be easily imputed into the hippocampus. A woman, on the other hand, is looking for a personal connection for the information, so it can be processed in the cerebral cortex.

There have been a host of arguments, misunderstandings, and accusations in many marriages over asking for directions, giving directions, doing a budget, staying within a budget, balancing the checkbook, maintaining cars, travel plans, precise wording, and a lot of other ways that men and women can fail to understand each other in this arena.

Sexuality

An area that strongly impacts marital relations is the sexual experience and the different ways men and women approach the experience. Sax notes that researchers found significant differences between the sexes in how they experienced and processed the sexual element of marriage. "Women's sexuality tends to be strongly linked to a close relationship. For women, an important goal of sex is intimacy; the best context for pleasurable sex is a committed relationship. This is less true for men."[7] The research found that men did not view sexuality through closeness of relationship but usually had an aggressive dimension to their sexual expression that was not at all true for women.[8]

As I have stated more fully in other books (*Becoming a Godly Wife* and *Mission Possible: Winning the Battle over Temptation*), men have sexual cycles similar to women, but they are timed differently. Women have a cycle that lasts approximately 28 days. They are physiologically programmed to be interested in sexual intercourse one time during a twenty-eight day cycle. Men have a completely different cycle. Every day the typical man produces between 100 million and 200 million sperm. When this number reaches 400-500 million, it needs to be released. That need for release triggers all kinds of physiological and psychological impulses for sexual intercourse in men. Therefore, a man is motivated to have sexual contact every 2-5 days compared to the average woman who is motivated to have sexual contact at only one time during the month. This difference can create great tension in the marriage. Husbands and wives must come to an understanding of this significant difference and to an agreement in its application.[9]

Healthy marriages work hard at meeting the man's recurring need for sexual relations. The need can be met by any one of three general types of sexual encounters. The first I call "WOW encounters," where both partners are interested and fully involved in pleasuring and being pleasured. Such encounters usually happen about once a month. Most men have a hard time understanding why these encounters cannot happen all the time because they are always interested. The second type I call "normal encounters." It is when a full sexual interaction takes place, but the woman usually is not hungry for the interaction. This type of encounter in the average marriage takes place once a week to twice a month. The third type of sexual connection in marriage I call a "quickie encounter." This is where only the man is fully engaged in the sexual episode, and his wife is merely ministering to his need. This third type of encounter may occur one to three times a week, depending upon the man.

Interest in Physical Violence

Men and women also respond differently to images of physical violence. Sax reasons that because of innate differences between boys and girls, boys use fighting and physical response as a tool for friendship and prioritization. "[Psychologist Janet Lever] found that boys who fight each other usually end up being better friends after the fight. They are more likely to play together in the days after the fight than they were in the days before."[10] Women and girls, however, do not fight physically but verbally and when driven to verbal fighting, the relationship often ends.

As a general rule, men don't see a problem with physical aggressiveness and violence like most women do. They are prone to situations in which physical threats or physical acts are conducted. These differences are real and can explain many problems men and women have in their discussions, recreational pursuits, and places where they are comfortable. Men often feel more comfortable where physical tension and physical solutions will be needed. Women are more comfortable where verbal wrestling and emotional tension are the norm. Men are drawn to action movies and physical sports such as football. Women are drawn to emotional movies and verbal sparring. A woman can handle a higher level of emotional tension, and a man can handle a higher level of physical tension. This does not in any way excuse a man from resorting to physical violence, but it may help his wife understand why he can't handle emotional interactions without leaving or being tempted to physical action.

A related idea, as Sax notes, is that men and boys consistently prefer action to emotions, whereas women and girls consistently prefer complex fictional stories full of emotional dilemmas and interesting motives.[11]

Stress: Acetylcholine vs. Adrenaline

One of the most fascinating differences between men and women is the different hormones released under stress and confrontation.

The following quotes reveal shocking differences between men and women when they are under significant stress.

The female autonomic nervous system has been shown to be influenced more by the parasympathetic nervous system, which is energized by acetylcholine rather than adrenaline, which causes an unpleasant nauseated feeling rather than the "thrill" of the sympathetic nervous system.[12]

When most young boys are exposed to threat and confrontation, their senses sharpen and they feel an exciting tingle. When most young girls are exposed to threat and confrontation, they feel dizzy and yucky. They may have unaccustomed trouble expressing themselves with just the right words. They may experience nausea or urge to use the bathroom.[13]

This same hormonal difference when exposed to stress is evident in marriage. A man under stress is secreting adrenaline, which tends to make him sharper and more confident. A woman under stress is subject to effects of acetylcholine, which can often bring nausea and dizziness. This combination often causes a woman to be more sensitive to stress and a man more willing to carry stress. This has huge implications for the individuals in a marriage handling debt, job loss, children, and disagreements. That is not to say it is good for a man to seek out stress. He is naturally drawn to it, for it releases more adrenaline and thereby makes him sharper. Many men today are overdosing on adrenaline, and they burn out because of it. Notice that the same stimuli can produce different results in men and women. That is a key insight.

This also means that in a fight or tense situation, a woman will be under the influence of a hormone that slows down her ability to respond, and a man will be under the influence of a hormone that causes him to respond more quickly and with clearer thought processes.

Nurturing

Another significant difference that Sax notes from the research between men and women is that females show a greater interest in nurturing their young than males do.

Whenever you look among the primates, you'll find that young females show more interest than young males do in taking care of babies…It is also true for humans: girls, on average, are much more likely to embrace little babies and be interested in babies than boys are. …Sons whose parents encourage them to nurture babies are no more nurturing than sons of parents who make no such efforts."[14]

Ancient roles in marriage had females caring for the children and offering the greatest amount of nurturing. This seems to be an innate response to internal impulses and not social conditioning. While it is possible to suppress this natural desire to nurture, the meaning, interest, and satisfaction in the nurturing cannot be denied.

Handling Aggression Differently

Another fascinating difference between the genders is how they use or avoid aggression. Males enjoy aggression and use it to explore friendships. One of the consistent ways that males establish friendships is through aggressive play or competition. That is not how women and girls establish friendships.

A number of men have let me know that they tried to be their wife's friend through all the normal channels and were punished for the effort. They tried teasing, wrestling, being aggressive, and playing rougher games, but the women did not respond positively. For men, aggression equals fun, but with girls aggression destroys relationships and this difference has strongly impacted many marriages.[15]

How many marriages have been destroyed by a wife's taking her husband's teasing in the wrong way? A man needs to be willing to turn off this aggressive teasing when he is at home. With every such attempt at friendship, he drives his wife further away. Men must understand that this is not the way women bond. Women must understand that men want to establish a close relationship of mutual banter, and their comments are not meant as personal attacks.

Friendships

Another significant difference between men and women is how they develop and maintain friendships. Sax notes that women and girls center friendships on conversation and communication. Men and boys center friendships on common activity. Notice what the research states:

> We might characterize the differences this way: girls' friendships are face to face—two or three girls talking with one another. Boys' friendships are shoulder to shoulder, a group of boys looking out at some common interest. [16]

Conversation is central to girls' friendships at every age. Girls love to talk with each other. When they start having trouble talking, the friendship is in trouble. The mark of a truly close friendship between two girls or two women is that they tell each other secrets they don't tell anyone else. They confide in each other about their most personal doubts and difficulties. Self-disclosure is the most precious badge of friendship between females. When she tells you a secret she's never told anyone else, you know you are truly her dear friend. Boys are different. Most boys don't really want to hear each other's innermost secrets. With boys the focus is on the activity, not the conversation.[17]

Finally, Sax notes that men and women have different reactions to stress in their friendships. Women want to be with their friends when they are under stress, while men usually want to be isolated when they are going through a stressful time.[18] Consider the impact of those facts on your marriage relationship. If you want your husband to be your best friend, there must be lots of time doing activities that he enjoys, and when he is under stress, he does not want initially to talk about it. If you want your wife to be your best friend, you must have lots of conversation and interactive communication.

Summary

Men and women are different in a number of ways. They are not just slightly different but completely different. Every cell of a man's body is different from every cell of a woman's body. Neither is right or wrong; they are both built to accomplish different purposes. They are also built to need each other in different ways. Husbands and wives must make the conscious decision to accept their spouses in all their wonderful differences. Enjoy it!

Marriage Solutions and Exercises:

- Which of the male and female differences mentioned in this section were the most eye opening to you?

- Which of the male and female differences in this section have contributed to the most disagreements, fights, or hurt feelings?

- Having read through the various physiological differences between men and women, what three questions would you like to ask your spouse?
  - o 1.
  - o 2.
  - o 3.

Various Temperament Assessments

There are a variety of temperament tests that analyze human behavior through different grids. None of these tests is perfect, nor are they a complete evaluation of a person's behavior. The value of these temperament tests is to help you identify the strong internal impulses that you and your spouse regularly feel. It also helps bring clarity to the impulses you and your spouse rarely feel. It is amazing to watch partners realize their spouse feels an internal nudge in a different direction from theirs. It isn't right or wrong; it just feels wrong because it's felt differently. It explains a lot when you understand that your spouse feels an internal impulse completely different from yours. There are hundreds of these internal impulses that, if consistently acted upon, will become habitual patterns of behavior. Within marriage, two different people are responding to the same situation with two different sets of internal impulses. Understanding these two sets of internal impulses often explains what is happening in the marriage.

It is possible to predict that one person will have a certain reaction to a given situation almost every time because of how he or she is wired. The internal impulses will push the person in a certain direction. Embrace the fact that your spouse will respond in the usual way. Great marriages happen when both partners come to the place of accepting the other. Getting mad, disappointed, or irritated will not change one's typical reaction. Your spouse feels certain internal impulses that propel him or her in a certain direction.

Myers-Briggs Temperament Types

Nancy could not understand Rafe. She was an introvert who enjoyed her home and two close friends. She was more than willing to go to church, but after the service she wanted to go home. She felt energized by the comfort of her own home. She always felt drained by being with a lot of people. Rafe, on the other hand, was an extrovert who loved large groups of people. The longer he was at church, the more he wanted to be there. He always sought out more people to be around. During dating those natural opposite tendencies excited and drew the couple together. After a few years of marriage, however, it was no longer enjoyable to be pulled in a direction contrary to one's personality. Nancy and Rafe got into several fights over this. Nancy always thought it was time to leave right after church, but Rafe never did. It took a long time for him to convince Nancy that he was wired differently than she was. He obtained energy from people and was drained by silence and solitude. She was the exact opposite. She loved the quietness of her home; especially when the children were at school. Reading a book, gardening, and general cleaning in the stillness of her own home were like heaven to her.

Their marriage began to take a turn for the better when they started taking two cars to church and social gatherings. Nancy could leave after a half hour. Rafe could stay with the children and be energized. When Rafe and the children returned, satiated by people, Nancy had been energized by her quiet time.

One of the most widely used temperament assessment tools is called the Myers-Briggs Type Indicator, which sorts people on four different scales:

- The Extroversion – Introversion Scale
- The Intuition – Sensation Scale

- The Thinking – Feeling Scale
- The Judging – Perceiving Scale

General ideas about this temperament assessment have been adapted from the book, *Do What You Are,* by Paul D. Tieger and Barbara Barron-Tieger.[19] Let's examine these four scales in more detail.

The Extroversion – Introversion Scale:

Extrovert ----------------------|-------------------- **Introvert**

This scale rates the level of energy you gain from being with others. The person high in extroversion gains energy from being with other people. The person high in introversion gains energy by being alone. Neither source of energy is right or wrong; different people gain energy in different ways. Unfortunately, it is easy to project onto your spouse that his or her preferences are wrong because they are different from yours. This kind of judgmental assessment is what I address in this chapter.

The person who is high in introversion is drained of energy approximately 30 minutes into a party and is ready to go home to re-energize. The person high in extroversion is just getting warmed up after 30 minutes. The longer that person is at the party, the more energy he or she feels. These two types of people often marry each other, which sets up all kinds of disagreements about how long to stay and how involved to become. In the story of Nancy and Rafe, it took him a long time to grasp that his wife really was drained from being around a lot of people. He just couldn't understand that what energized him drained her.

Sometimes introversion and extroversion can be situational, and that must be taken into account. Some people act like introverts in certain situations in that they are drained by interactions with people and prefer to have deeper conversations with only a few. Some people act like extroverts in certain situations when they are energized by the people in the room and want to talk with everyone. I have known a number of people who become functional extroverts when they are in charge of or are the focus of a gathering, even though their basic personality preference is introversion.

The Intuition – Sensation Scale:

Intuitive ----------------------|---------------------- **Sensate**

This scale rates one's preference for dealing with abstraction or actual objects. The person who is high in intuition prefers to deal with abstract concepts, ideas, and nuances. The person who is high in sensation prefers to deal with actual things, people, and situations. This scale has been described as what a person enjoys focusing on, either what is or what could be. Those on one side of the scale are called sensors. They prefer gathering data through the five senses. They have an internal trust and attraction for what can be measured, documented, seen, tasted, smelled, or touched. Those who have this preference have a natural internal focus on what is happening right now in the real world.

Those who are high on the intuitive side of the scale are called intuitives. Intuitives look for meaning, patterns, or the big picture and live primarily in the future. Intuitives consistently try to read between the lines. They seek to interpret meaning and possibilities. Intuitives are more excited about future possibilities and the need for change.[20]

The person who is high in intuition wants to interact with abstract ideas of justice, righteousness, fairness, and peace. The person who is a sensor wants to know who and what we are talking about. When I've worked with couples that have huge disparities in this area, I have to remind the intuitives to start with a concrete person and a concrete situation. That helps the sensor engage in the conversation. While the sensor talks, the intuitive must realize that present realities are central, and the sensor does not want to find hidden meaning behind the words. He or she wants to continue talking about the actual situation without broadening the discussion to universal principles. For marriage to work, there must be lots of bending and communication and acceptance and deferment to each other.

These obvious differences in preference between the real and the possible can easily cause a couple to talk past each other on a wide variety of subjects. I have watched significant harm done to a marriage because negative judgments were made about the other person's orientation. Be very careful that you do not judge the other person's natural perspective with comments like the following:

- "You never do anything practical that will really help us; you are always dreaming and scheming!"

- "You have no creativity and imagination. I don't know if I can live with someone who is so stupid!"

- "Get your head out of the clouds and do something that has value!"

- "How could you not see the powerful themes in that movie?"

Realize both perspectives are needed and valuable. Our world and your marriage need practical, real world vision and planning, dreaming, and behind the lines understanding. If two people can use differences in a positive teamwork process, they can be better together than either individual alone. Each can realize the truth of what the other says even though it feels like a foreign language. It is also important to realize that everyone uses both orientations, but this scale measures preferences.

The Thinking – Feeling Scale:

Thinking --------------------|--------------------- Feeling

This scale rates a person's preference for making decisions either from a distant or a personal position. The thinker prefers to get the facts of a situation and then pull back and consider options from a more objective position. The feeler prefers decisions to be shaped by immediate reactions, emotions, and interplay with others. Neither preference is wiser or more intelligent than the other; both approaches may be intelligent in certain situations and both may be foolish in certain situations. There is a natural tendency to believe your own preference is the best way.

Thinkers prefer to make linear and logical decisions that are derived from factual realities with little or no emotional factors. Thinkers enjoy putting themselves outside the situation to make an objective decision. They want to make decisions as though they had no personal feelings in the decision. They enjoy analyzing a situation from this distant, unemotional, detached position. The power for the thinker is in the clarity of the logic with little or no concern for the feelings those conclusions might produce.[21]

On the other hand, feelers prefer to make decisions based upon emotional reactions and personal interplay that a decision will produce. They approach a situation mentally asking, "What will happen if we make this decision? How will this person respond to this decision?" Feelers have an uncanny ability to anticipate emotional reactions to decisions because they automatically play them out in their minds beforehand. Feelers are able to be more empathetic and compassionate as they make decisions based upon their understanding of the future emotional and mental responses of others.

Both thinking and feeling preferences are essential in the world. The linear world of the thinker allows for buildings to be built, projects to be envisioned, and hard decisions to be made. The emotional world of the feeler creates healthy relationships and anticipates real world interactions. Feelers allow for groups to form teams that work and for political parties to be more than one-issue groups. They are more adept at the art of people skills, but they can be bogged down by the emotions they accurately sense and predict. Thinkers naturally cut through the emotional clutter and accurately outline needed changes and strategies.[22] As the Tiegers point out on the negative side, "Thinkers can be analytical to the point of seeming cold, and Feelers can be personally involved to the point of seeming overemotional."[23]

This is the only one of the four temperament assessments that has gender bias. About two thirds of men are thinkers, and about two thirds of women are feelers. That is most likely why we think women are generally more emotional.

I have watched misunderstandings of these two internal temperament impulses destroy harmony in a marriage. A husband might make a logical plan for Christmas—whose house to go to and who to buy gifts for. But he fails to take into account the emotional reaction of the people who will be affected by his plan. If he asserts his plan without input from his feeler wife, he may alienate his family, upset his wife, break down the relationship between grandparents and his kids, and possibly impact his inheritance. His logical plan does not take into account traditions, feelings, reactions, family culture, and a host of other things that his feeling wife could help him understand. On the other hand, a feeling wife may instinctively make a number of impulsive purchases to make others happy. She does not realize the money she used was saved for new tires or another budgetary item that will be needed later. In her mind, the short-term positive emotional reaction of the people involved is worth it! Besides, the money can always be replaced.

The Judging – Perceiving Scale:

Judging ---------------------------|-------------------- **Perceiving**

This scale rates a person's preference for closure or continued process. People who rank high on judging prefer closure and settling things. Those who rank high in perceiving prefer to keep their options open and to delay making decisions for the sake of spontaneity. This temperament analysis tries to measure the internal desire for closure or spontaneity. Again, the labels assigned to these assessments can have a negative connotation for some. But in this instance, "judging" does not mean a condemning attitude or judgmental perspective; it means the desire to make decisions and achieve certainty. Neither preference is right or wrong. Both are helpful.

Judgers have a natural preference for order, structure, and decisions. They prefer to make decisions rather than leave things undecided. They tend to abhor what is unplanned and unstructured. They have an internal delight and happiness when there is a place for everything and when everything is in its place. They prefer to regulate and control the life they live with predictable patterns. Decisions are not difficult, and they feel relieved when they're made. They feel uncomfortable when a decision has not been made. Judgers will press for a resolution of issues because they like things to be resolved. They sense an internal pressure to resolve issues and cannot rest until that has taken place, which tends to make them appear coldhearted.[24]

Perceivers like to keep their options open. They like to shoot from the hip and leave a little room for the unknown and the unplanned.

Those who have this preference are uncomfortable with too much rigidity and predictability. They need room to live and breathe. They enjoy not knowing what will happen. They are often happiest when their lives are the most flexible. Their perspective is that they want to stay open to all options and that any decision that closes down options is negative. Perceivers like to "go with the flow." They want to understand how life works more than control it. They are able to perceive options that others might not, and they want all those options to remain viable as long as possible. [25]

An important distinction between Judgers and Perceivers is the issue of closure. Judgers experience tension until closure is reached and are constantly drawn toward making a decision. Perceivers, on the other hand, experience tension when they are forced to make a decision; they avoid closure and prefer to keep their options open.[26]

This temperament preference has created hundreds of fights between couples. Opposites in this area attract, so the Bohemian artist marries the buttoned-down executive. The detailed neat-nick marries the "whatever" slob. One partner pushes for a decision regarding vacations, schools for the kids, arrangement of the living room, and future employment only to have the laid-back processor delay making a decision as long as possible. Sometimes resistance to making a decision causes the laid-back person to wait until it is too late and his or her nondecision becomes a decision. One must realize that the perceiving person needs more facts to make the best decision. That is the only way to speed up the ability to make a decision.

Summary

There are a number of issues to note about these. Some are more appropriate at certain times than others. All of us at times will have to function outside our preferences if we are to be successful. We must accept that others prefer to follow impulses different from ours. We must not worry about how we came to agree, only that we get along. We must accept the patterns and preferences in our spouse and not try to change them. Many of these deep-seated preferences are unchanging. Marriage is a wonderful laboratory for different people to try to get along and to be loving at the same time.

Marriage Solutions and Exercises:

- Which of the Myers–Briggs Temperament scales mentioned in this section were the most eye opening to you?

- Which of the Myers–Briggs Temperament scales in this section have contributed to the most disagreements, fights, or hurt feelings?

- Having read through the Myers–Briggs Temperament scales, what three questions would you like to ask your spouse in regard to these differences?
  - o 1.
  - o 2.
  - o 3.

Four Ancient Temperament Types

To Diana, it seemed as if Jerry was about to lose control whenever he got angry. And it seemed as if he was always angry. She was a flexible, amiable person who had a pleasant disposition most of the time. She married Jerry because he knew what he wanted and went after it with gusto. He was confident and in charge. What Diana didn't realize was that a strong need for control was welded to his leadership abilities. That meant he was not very flexible with his expectations. Jerry had struggled with anger his whole life because he tended to turn desires into expectations. Even after working with his expectations and improving significantly, his anger lay just beneath the surface. Many times his emotions flared. Diana needed to realize that Jerry would never be as easygoing as she was. What made him a great leader also made him more prone to anger. It was also true that without lots of work, his anger would destroy his marriage.

Thankfully, Jerry put in the time to learn how to manage his expectations and his reactions. Jerry needed to work on controlling his aggression and anger; Diana needed to embrace Jerry's different orientation to life and expectations.

There is an ancient temperament test that divides mankind into four basic groupings. It was originally proposed during the flowering of the Greek civilization and has seen many updates and revisions. This ancient personality assessment groups a number of temperament impulses and choices. While it is not an exact science, it is helpful to understand that certain temperament impulses tend to group together. The reason for exploring this material is not to predict how others may act but to realize that others experience completely different internal impulses. These impulses are not right or wrong, but rather they are how your past, your internal wiring, and your choices constantly advise you.

Florence Littauer has produced a number of books, seminars, and materials that help explain the four ancient temperament types. She does an excellent job of applying the truths of these insights to practical problems and real people. A number of people have found her books especially helpful.[27]

The four basic temperament drives have been described in various ways:

- Sanguine, Choleric, Phlegmatic, and Melancholy
- Expressive, Driver, Amiable, and Analytic
- Otters, Lions, Golden Retrievers, and Beavers
- Dominant, Influencing, Steady, and Compliant.

While different expressions of temperament offer slightly different perspectives, they each view the basic temperaments in the same way. I tend to see them as clustering around four different dominant internal impulses: popularity, power, peace, and perfect.

Popularity

People who predominate with this internal temperament impulse have the need to be noticed. They are often loud, boisterous, spontaneous, and gregarious in order to be noticed. They have a need to be popular and the center of attention. It usually means that they dress to be noticed. They develop habits of speech, manner, and style so they will be noticed. The internal impulse to be popular means they have a need to be liked, which moves them to discover quite quickly many of the essential people skills. They know how to focus their attention on a person and make that person feel as if he or she is the only person in the world. They know how to tell a story so that people are captivated as it unfolds. These people are natural speakers, sales persons, and actors.

On the other hand, they do not like to be in the background. They do not gain any satisfaction from planning and behind-the-scenes work. They are de-energized by a lack of attention. Their temperament impulses usually are accompanied by negative traits like forgetfulness and susceptibility to temptation. They can become angry quickly and be over it just as quickly in order to remain popular. They can appear fickle as the fads and flows of what makes a person popular change.

People who are married to this type of person must not try to help them mature by holding them back from their childish need for popularity and self-seeking, but they should instead help them meet the need for attention in a positive and appropriate way. This spouse must leave room for his or her partner to be the center of attention in some positive way. The popular type needs social interaction and engagement just as he needs to breathe and eat. The spouse of the popular person must let him or her be popular and socially engaged. The spouse cannot imprison him or her in the home or family duties and expect the spouse to be satisfied. Being social is not being unfaithful.

Power

The person who feels the internal impulse to be powerful needs to be in control. Such people are the most natural leaders in that they instinctively know what to do to become the person in charge. Everyone wants to get his own way, but this person internally feels the need to get his own way and will do far more than people with the other temperaments. Others will usually bow to the unbending will of this individual because the ferocity of his or her declarations and movements makes yielding easier. With this temperament impulse there is usually a bias for action through which one's power and control can be asserted and increased.

These people can be restless for action and ill prepared to be good team players if they are not in charge. Their anger can be white-hot and almost unquenchable until they gain the ascendancy. They are often belligerently stubborn and want to win an argument even if they know they are wrong. That can lead to character assaults and various techniques to make sure they do not lose arguments.

People married to this type of person must realize that their spouse has a strong need for power and control and that his or her natural gifts at leadership should be encouraged not discouraged. Their leadership, power, and action are needed in the marriage and in our world in some place, and they must be appreciated and helped to express their temperament in God-honoring ways. If they are bottled up and not allowed to use their abilities and temperament impulses, they will blow up and use them in a destructive way.

Peace

The person with the natural impulse and understanding of how to bring about peace perceives the words, actions, attitudes, and directions that need to be taken to maintain harmony and peace. This person often will sacrifice his or her own interests, time, and even popularity to make everyone get along. They are valuable people, who do not seek the limelight, nor do they want to be noticed; they just want peace. This temperament impulse usually comes with an amiability and flexibility that everyone finds enjoyable. This person is everyone's friend and no one's enemy. He or she absorbs the energy, direction, and attitude of others and can subtly redirect or recast it to work with the energy, direction, and attitude of others.

Peacemakers do not work fast, but they remain flexible and deliberate so they can always respond to the peaceful impulse. Because they are oriented to peace, they are maintainers of the status quo and are not change agents. They are reluctant leaders and excel only when they have energetic leaders below them whose ideas, energy, and action they can redirect. They can appear as lazy and dull because they are aware of how any change can disrupt the present peace.

The peacemaker's spouse must realize that such a person will never be an initiating leader with lots of ideas and lots of action. The spouse must learn to trust the peacemaker's suggestions and amiability. He or she must respect that this person needs the most time to deal with change. Usually one person in the marriage is stronger and more action-oriented, and the peace-oriented person is seeking to polish, redirect, and defang the action-oriented partner. Some of this should be allowed, for it is helpful, but usually one can never be as peaceful as the peaceful person desires. Change must take place, and disruptions are a part of that, so we must give this person time to deal with the disruption.

Perfect

People who internally feel the need to be perfect drive themselves and others toward that goal relentlessly. Everything they do is usually explained or driven by this motive. These people seem to know instinctively how to do everything the "right" way. They are irritated with themselves and others when this standard is not achieved. They will need to check and recheck, do and redo, a project until it is as close to perfection as they can make it. And even then they will be more aware of the flaws than the strengths. Usually, this temperament impulse comes with a high intellectual capacity. They are usually highly creative and gifted musically and artistically in many cases without training. This type of person can excel at almost any task that confronts him or her because he or she quickly grasps what is required to do a job perfectly and feels an internal drive to accomplish that level. This temperament impulse also is willing to make deep personal sacrifice for friends and loved ones that are beyond what others usually are willing to make. This person finds joy in the smallest job or assignment when it is performed perfectly.

People animated by this perfection impulse come with a number of weaknesses also. They can be moody, sullen, and depressed, maybe because of their own lack of perfect achievement. They can be or border on being obsessive compulsive about almost everything in their life. If there is a right way of doing something, they know what it is and cannot perform below that standard. That can cause life to be a constant series of all-out sprints in each relational arena.

People who are married to others with these perfection impulses must realize the height of their standard and move as far in that direction as prudence will allow. The spouse must also make room for their creativity and need for artistic expression. They must expect deep negative mood swings and stop asking their mate to turn off the melancholy emotional feelings. God made these people with this strength, and they have a unique contribution to make to your marriage and to the world. Life will never be as perfect as they want, but it can be improved.

Remember that each of us feels internal impulses that feel "right" to us. Most people are a mixture of two of the above temperament impulses in which one predominates, and the other is present but not as strong as the first. We are true to our best selves when we follow these impulses appropriately. It is very easy to see your spouse's different impulses as wrong or destructive instead of realizing that God made marriage about two people getting along to rear children, attain financial stability, and maintain community coherence. People who have opposite impulses often seem attracted to each other and eventually marry. Leave room for your spouse's different internal impulses and become a powerful team instead of remaining as selfish individuals.

Marriage Exercise

- Which of the Ancient Temperament impulses mentioned in this section is the most representative of you? Of your spouse?

- Which of the Ancient Temperament assessments in this section has contributed to the most disagreements, fights, or hurt feelings?

- Having read through the Ancient Temperament assessments, what three questions would you like to ask your spouse in regard to these differences?
  o 1.
  o 2.
  o 3.

The Five Love Languages

John felt the best way to express his love was to show it in a tangible way. He looked for ways to serve Helen so she would know how much he loved her. Helen, however, felt the best way to express love was to spend time and show interest in each other's favorite things.

It took a while for John to realize that Helen was not impressed by his work around the house. He never had time to take her out or to watch her favorite TV program with her; he was too busy trying to show her he loved her. She, on the other hand, invited John to participate with her in social activities and trips she wanted to take so she could love him. These differences in what are known as love languages created some rocky moments in their marriage. Once they realized they truly loved each other but expressed and received love in different ways, their marriage improved.

Some marriages break up because the husband or wife can't express or receive love unless it is his or her preferred method. In those instances, husbands and wives feel unloved even though their spouse is trying desperately to communicate that love.

Another temperament assessment tool refers to the way people prefer to give and receive love. Psychologists have discovered that people love others in five distinct ways. Gary Chapman has written extensively on this phenomenon in *The Five Love Languages.*[28] The discussions here are echoes of his fine work in this area.

Each one of us has a preference for giving and receiving love in one or two of these languages. When two people are speaking the same love language, the messages are sent and received more clearly. If, however, someone tries to communicate his love for another person in one language, and she prefers to be loved in a different language, the message is garbled. I have watched marriages experience huge "aha" moments when husbands and/or wives realize what their partner was trying to say. In fact, many spouses have been upset with their mates while the mate was trying to communicate love. The understanding of these simple languages will allow you to communicate love much more clearly. The five basic love languages are acts of service, physical touch and closeness, gift giving, quality time, and words of encouragement. Here are brief descriptions, so you can identify your spouse's and your basic preferences in love languages.[29]

Acts of Service

The person with a preference for giving and receiving love through serving feels best when love is expressed through tangible acts of service. This person is more likely to offer to baby-sit, fix a fence, give a ride, or take care of your animals. He or she feels most comfortable expressing love in a tangible way. This person also feels the most loved when others express love to him or her in this way.[30]

Tami was a person who served everyone and had tons of friends. But what really didn't make sense to her was how people returned her friendship. They wanted to talk with her, bring her gifts, invite her to fancy dinner parties, and offer big hugs, but very few wanted to help her with her projects. If they really loved her, that is what they should do, she thought. Even her husband was reluctant to do projects to demonstrate his love for Tami because there were too many projects, and no one could keep up with her level of service. It took time to help Tami see that not everyone was wired the way she was. Her husband and friends were not letting her down. They weren't unloving. They just had different love languages. She was speaking Chinese, and they were speaking Russian, French, and German. Even thinking about speaking Chinese as Tami did seemed too difficult for them.

I know a man who expressed his love through acts of service. At one point in his life he met the woman of his dreams and tried to get her to notice him. He began listening carefully for ways that she might need help, so he could display his love for her. When she needed her car repaired, he volunteered. When she had trouble with her home, he was the first to volunteer to fix it. When she needed something done for a project at church, he was right there to help. It was his way of saying, "I love you." At first, she didn't understand all this extra attention, and it caught her off guard. Because he was not romancing her in the way she was expecting, she was not moved by his overtures of love. Eventually, he was able to adapt to her need for quality time, which revealed that he was interested. Then she was told about love languages and understood what his service to her was about. She got the message, and they married.

Physical Touch and Closeness

People who prefer to love and be loved through physical touch need to touch and be close to the people they care about. These people have been described as affectionate and touchy-feely. They need to touch to make sure that how much they care is understood. This is the person who needs five hugs a day. This is the person who naturally reaches out to touch a shoulder. This is the person who offers hugs for comfort. He or she gives and receives love most strongly through physical touch and closeness. When such a person thinks about receiving love, it involves touch and closeness.[31]

One of my daughters uses this love language. She needs to be held, touched, and cuddled a lot. She stands near me so she can touch me. She holds on to me and wants to be in physical contact with me as much as possible. I suspect her husband will enjoy the closeness when they are married. I'm sure I will be very careful when she starts spending time with boyfriends so she does not express too much too soon. Many marriages would be greatly improved if there were more cuddling and hugging if one or both partners have this love language as their primary or secondary love language. Realize that if a man has a need for physical touch and closeness, his desire and hunger for sexual encounters will be even more frequent than the normal male. If your husband or wife makes a regular habit out of hugging you to show appreciation or approval, you must adjust to this love language. Even if you don't have a need for much contact, minister to your spouse's way of being loved.

Gift-Giving

People who prefer to give and receive love through gift giving have the uncanny ability to know what gift would really light up another person's world. Special gifts that you don't even remember mentioning are what people with this love language remember. Since it comes so easily to them, they can expect others to know what gift they really want. The gifts they give are not always expensive; they just hit the spot and communicate love and uniqueness to the recipient. People find themselves exclaiming, "How did you know?" when a person with this gift touches their lives.[32]

My wife has a very close friend who clearly has this love language. She seems to know instinctively what gifts to give our girls that truly please them. She is not particularly a warm and cuddly person, but she communicates bucketfuls of love through her specific gift giving. Love is tangible for this person.

We all know couples that have huge problems at Christmas, anniversaries, and birthdays because one of the partners gives lame gifts that say, "I didn't spend much time thinking about this special occasion." One couple started a fight on Christmas day that lasted three weeks over the insensitivity and inexpensive nature of the gifts. Without a real understanding of the differences in love languages, some couples that are full of love start heading down the road to divorce court.

Quality Time

The person who prefers to give and receive love through quality time sees love as special time doing a cherished activity. It is through the mutual enjoyment of an activity or interest that love is shared and expanded for this person. When someone of this bent feels or expresses love, it is the quality of the time, the depth of the interaction, and the interest in the activity that communicates love. People with this love language are often private people who save their favorite hobby, activity, or interests for those they want to be closest to. It can be devastating if those who profess to love this person refuse to go to his or her event, ridicule the activity he or she is attracted to, or dismiss the hobby that enthralls him or her.[33]

I watched one couple have a really difficult time making their marriage work because the wife regularly criticized her husband's hobbies. She would make comments like, "You go ahead and play with your trains, and I will do important things like taking care of the children," or "Why would I want to go down to an old warehouse and watch a bunch of grown men spend endless hours wasting time on stupid trains?" You can imagine it didn't take long for that husband to shut his wife out of his emotional life. He had offered her the key to his heart by inviting her to watch him operate his beloved trains, but she refused and rejected his love. She would tell you that he is a cold and introverted man who is unloving. But that is not true. I've watched him light up and become almost bombastic when he is in the train yard describing his trains. Interestingly enough, this woman didn't want my help—she just wanted agreement that her husband wasn't a romantic. She never realized that the romance of his life involved trains, and he had invited her to share in this romantic life.

I know a man who saw his marriage take a huge leap forward when he and his wife sat down to make a list of dates they could go on once a month. Many of the dates were things he deeply enjoyed. The fact that she would enjoy them with him spoke volumes of her love for him. That she was willing to go to football games and active sports activities ministered to the depth of his heart. It was, therefore, easy for him to go on dates that filled up the romantic places in her heart.

Words of Encouragement

People who prefer this path of giving and receiving love are full of encouragement and crave the same. Such people are able to say the encouraging thing in almost any situation. Love is communicated through words. If there is not a constant banter of respect, potential, hope, and care, there isn't love in the relationship. This person craves verbal encouragement. Most people need compliments every day, but this person craves compliments. Without them, he will doubt whether he is loved. Pay attention to see if your spouse naturally gives compliments to others. If your spouse does, he or she may have this love language.[34]

I know of a woman who lights up every time her husband specifically mentions things she has done well. It is like rain falling on a thirsty flowerbed. It is generally a good idea to give your spouse a compliment every day. When you find that your spouse drinks in these compliments, increase it to two or three a day. No one ever overdosed on genuine, specific compliments. Just start noticing things your spouse does for the family, for you, for his or her company, or for the community. If you start to take notice, you will see more. In response, there will be more compliment-worthy actions toward you.

Summary

The Five Love Languages are a proven way to talk about some of the nuances of love. As you come to understand your spouse's love language, you will increase your ability to love your spouse. If a person generally gives a particular form of love, he or she will speak and receive love in that same language. If you don't speak your partner's dominant love language very well, practice! Work at it, so your marriage does not die for lack of love when it is all around.

Marriage Solutions and Exercises

- Which of the Five Love Languages represents you? Your spouse?

- Which of the Five Love Languages has contributed to the most fights?

- Having read through the Five Love Languages assessments, what three questions would you like to ask your spouse about these differences?
  - o 1.
  - o 2.
  - o 3.

Summary of the Problem of Clashing Temperaments

If a marriage is going to work, it requires that both husband and wife accept the differences and personality of their spouse. It is essential that both partners come to terms with the different impulses and personality orientations that make their spouse who he or she is. Trying to change an unchangeable aspect of the other person is highly destructive to the marriage. The wonder of the marriage is in realizing that the two of you are now a team. A team can accomplish more together than either can apart. Both people have strengths and weaknesses, and they can be used to aid the marriage relationship, or they can form the basis for constant fighting. Learn how to look at your spouse's predictable patterns and accept them as strengths in the marriage. Partners do what they do in many cases because they are wired differently from their spouse.

The more that couples can take into account that the other person is a totally different being, the more that tolerance and acceptance can be extended to each other. As couples look at male and female differences, personality impulses, love languages, and other personality measures, they can see that their spouse feels different internal impulses than they do. When a couple incorporates these differences into their marriage in a functional way, the whole team is stronger.

Do not be secretly wishing that your mate's temperament were different, but instead embrace your spouse's unique personality and various unique behaviors as wonderful gifts. It is only in this way that a marriage can move forward toward healing.

The Five Problems of Marriage

Ignoring Needs	Immature Behaviors	Clashing Temperaments	Competing Relationships	Past Baggage
Wife's Needs Honor Understanding Security Building Unity Agreement Nurture Defender **Husband's Needs** Respect Adaptation Domestic Leadership Intimacy Companionship Attractive Soul and Body Listener	**Level 1** Thoughtless Immaturity **Level 2** Directed Immaturity **Level 3** Destructive, and/or Addictive Immaturity **Eight Solutions** Stop Further Immaturity Apology Alignment Thoughtful Requests More Love Change Behavior Clarify Patience	**Male vs. Female** **Myers-Briggs Temperament** **Ancient Temperament** **Love Languages**		

Dear Heavenly Father,

I want to confess to you that I have resented that my spouse does _____, and now I realize that this is a part of how you wired him/her on the inside. I love my wife/husband and choose to make room for this unchanging characteristic. I ask you to show me ways to accept the whole of who my spouse really is. Thank you for making him/her just as you did.

Problem #4

Competing Relationships

Problem #4

Competing Relationships

1 Timothy 3:4-7; John 19:26-27; 1 Timothy 5:8

Overview

Bill and Mary came into my office because they were headed for divorce. My office was their last stop before they called it quits. Their problem was really not their marriage; it was their children. Their children were out of control and disrupting everything. The kids were playing Dad against Mom and keeping the house in constant turmoil. The kids somehow knew if they could keep Mom and Dad fighting, they would never have to do anything they didn't want to do. They didn't realize their plan was working so well the family was about to split apart. Bill and Mary could not agree on how to handle the child crisis or how to raise the children in general. Bill wanted to be strict, and Mary wanted to be more loving and affirming. This parenting crisis led to constant fights and the potential dissolution of their marriage. They both agreed they loved each other; it was that they couldn't agree on how to raise the kids. They were about to get a divorce even though their marriage was fine.

I explained basic Marital Intelligence and the five problems of marriage. The fourth problem is competing relationships that drain the marriage of time, energy, and money. They were open to working on their marriage by working on their parenting. We spent our time together discussing a rational, biblical approach to parenting that would be effective and loving. As their parenting skills improved, so did their marriage. When Mom and Dad became an effective parenting team, a number of changes took place in the home. They stopped fighting about the kids, the children were brought under loving control, and their love for each other resurfaced. It took significant work for Bill and Mary to learn how to avoid being sucked into their children's manipulative distractions, but they practiced their new parenting skills until the family became a team.

Bill and Mary's situation is one example of what I have seen dozens of times in the counseling office. I call it competing relationships. Everyone has ten major relationships in his or her life. Those relationships all want more attention than we can give them, so they start competing with each other. Without a biblical priority structure, there will never be harmony between the various relationships in your life. When a couple gets married, they go through the honeymoon period in which both overlook almost everything to spend time on this new marriage relationship. At some point in the marriage, however, the other nine relationships will demand a huge new investment of time. Your business requires a lot of time to get it running. Your mother gets sick, and you are needed to help out. You lose your job, so money gets really tight while you look for another. Your involvement at church ramps up because it's summer. Your health takes a turn for the worse. You have a child who demands every minute of your attention. Your school load increases as you near the end. If you do not stay grounded with a biblical priority structure, you will be tempted to take the time that is needed to keep your marriage healthy and give it to one of the other relationships in your life. While all these are legitimate needs and pressures, be careful. These other relationships can suck all your time, energy, and resources so there will be nothing left for your marriage. Many people believe their marriage is supposed to survive whether or not there is any time, energy, or money given to it, but that is an unrealistic expectation.

A marriage requires a commitment of time, energy, and resources just to survive, let alone thrive and grow. No one would expect a garden to grow without a gardener giving it the proper care. But many people expect their marriage to grow and thrive without putting in time, energy, and money. Don't be foolish. Every single day you need to do some things that will strengthen your marriage. Therefore, if your schedule will not allow you to strengthen your marriage every single day, your schedule is too full.

The Fourth Element in Marital Intelligence

The fourth component of Marital Intelligence is Competing Relationships. It takes a commitment of time, energy, and resources to make a marriage thrive. It is very easy to allow the demands of our lives determine how we spend our time. Whatever screams the loudest usually gets the most time. If you live this way very long, it will destroy a vibrant marriage. The marital relationship won't cry out until it is in serious trouble. Your children will scream for more attention. Your checkbook will scream for more attention. Your career will demand more attention. Your hobbies need more attention to improve. Your church and civic involvements will ask for more time and focus. To combat this, you must work from a blueprint. To stay healthy and growing, your marriage needs a minimum of one hour a day of focused attention.

We have to make decisions on how we allot our time based upon our priorities, not upon who screams the loudest. To have a flourishing marriage we must say no to some good things. The difficulty comes when we must decline fascinating, interesting, and desirable people and activities to cultivate a great marriage.

Let me give you an estimate of the minimum time required to thrive in each major area of life. These are minimums. You may always add more time. Do not overcommit your time, so you have nothing to give in an emergency. Emergencies will arise in each relationship, and you must have time to give when crises come. One of today's traps is allowing our lives to spin faster and faster until there is not enough time for anything. I have watched with increasing dismay as people have committed themselves to huge amounts of time at work, church, or with their kids' athletic or artistic pursuits and then have no time for their marriage. When strains come on the marriage (and they will come), there is no time, no energy, and no resources to give. What usually results is a complete meltdown of the marriage.

Take the time to look at these minimums and put a *yes* by the relationships you are giving these minimums and a *no* by the relationships where you are giving less than the minimums. Realize that these are minimums, not maximums.

Relationship	Minimum amount of time to maintain health	Evaluate (Yes or No)
God	1+ hours per day	
Self	1-3 hours per day	
Marriage	1-2 hours per day	
Family	1-3 hours per day	
Work	8-10 hours per day	
Church	5 hours per week	
Money	1 hour per week	
Society	2 hours per month	
Friends	4 hours per week	
Enemies	1 hour per week	

A good marriage requires at least an hour a day of focused attention on each other. I do not believe it's possible to get around this minimum amount. What often happens is other relationships demand more hours, so we take them from the relationship that won't complain—our marriage. Before you know it, it's been weeks since you dated your spouse, days since you truly communicated, and weeks since you did something together you both enjoy. It may have been a year or more since you got away overnight without the kids in order to be a couple.

There are all kinds of ways to spend time with your spouse. Many of them were suggested in the previous sections on needs.

- Focused attention talking or listening
- Focused attention doing a project together

- Focused attention watching something side by side
- Focused attention participating in an event together
- Focused attention doing something for the other person
- Focused attention romantically and/or sexually
- Focused attention doing chores and projects

The key idea here is to focus on the other person and the meeting of his or her needs. When there is daily energy and love pouring into the marriage, it creates a better relational climate and allows for difficult times.

Marital Intelligence Test

This test probes the actions necessary to have a great marriage. Do not be surprised by the results. Celebrate your strengths and work on improving your weak areas. Your spouse might respond differently to the same questions. The areas of differences are opportunities to grow and improve your marriage. Hopefully, this test will whet your appetite for the solutions in this book.

Problem #4 0 = Never; 1 = Rarely; 2 = Occasionally; 3 = Sometimes; 4 = Usually; 5 = Always	
I encourage my spouse to have a strong relationship with God.	0 1 2 3 4 5
I help my spouse take time for himself/herself.	0 1 2 3 4 5
I take time for myself to be refreshed and rested.	0 1 2 3 4 5
I demonstrate that my spouse and our marriage are more important than our children.	0 1 2 3 4 5
I place my marriage and children ahead of my extended family.	0 1 2 3 4 5
I take time daily to get away from work and focus on my wife, family, and home life.	0 1 2 3 4 5
I make sure that we have vacations and family times.	0 1 2 3 4 5

I demonstrate that my marriage is more important than our church or charity involvements.	0 1 2 3 4 5
I am responsible in earning, managing, and giving our money.	0 1 2 3 4 5
I demonstrate that my marriage is more important than my community and/or civic involvements.	0 1 2 3 4 5
I put appropriate amounts of time into all the major arenas of my life.	0 1 2 3 4 5
I demonstrate that my marriage is more important than my friends.	0 1 2 3 4 5
I demonstrate that my marriage is more important than my competitors, enemies, bosses, and/or oppressors.	0 1 2 3 4 5
My spouse encourages me to have a strong relationship with God.	0 1 2 3 4 5
My spouse encourages me to be healthy spiritually, mentally, emotionally, and physically and to take time for myself.	0 1 2 3 4 5
My spouse demonstrates that our marriage is more important than our children.	0 1 2 3 4 5
My spouse puts our marriage and our children ahead of his/her extended family.	0 1 2 3 4 5
My spouse makes sure every day that he/she disengages from work and focuses for some period of time on our marriage, home, and family.	0 1 2 3 4 5
My spouse makes sure that we have vacations and family times.	0 1 2 3 4 5
My spouse demonstrates our marriage is more important than his/her church or charitable involvements.	0 1 2 3 4 5
My spouse is responsible in gaining, managing, and giving our money.	0 1 2 3 4 5

My spouse demonstrates that our marriage is more important than his/her community or civic involvements.	0 1 2 3 4 5
My spouse demonstrates that our marriage is more important than his/her friends.	0 1 2 3 4 5
My spouse demonstrates that our marriage is more important than his/her competitors, enemies, bosses, and/or oppressors.	0 1 2 3 4 5
My spouse puts an appropriate amount of time in all the major arenas of his/her life.	0 1 2 3 4 5
Subtotal Section #4	

How did you do? Remember that these results reflect the current condition of your relationship today. Realize, too, that no one is the perfect spouse. All of us have allowed other good relationships to squeeze out the time, energy, and resources we need for a thriving marriage; but with time and effort, your marriage can improve.

The positive statements on the test outline a high standard of how we should treat each other. Start applying these truths, and your relationship will improve right away.

Scoring

125 - 94: You have a very good marriage in this area. Keep it up. Have a discussion with your spouse about how to make sure that other relationships don't squeeze your marriage out.

93 - 62: You have a good marriage that could be significantly improved by planning and guarding your time together. Pick one thing you will stop and one new way to spend time together this month.

61 - 32: There are some serious deficiencies in the expression of love in your marriage. Both of you feel that you are being damaged by the lack of time and energy being put into your marriage. Some things will need to be eliminated to give your marriage a chance. Remember your marriage will not improve until there is more love flowing between husband and wife.

31 - 0: There is a lack of love in your marriage and significant selfishness. It takes only one person in the marriage to make a difference in the beginning. You need to learn new ways of living life in one or more relational arenas. The way you are living right now is not working for the health of your marriage.

Prioritized Relationships

Relationships must fit into a prioritized order if we are to have a healthy and functional life. We can't give our time, energy, and resources to whatever relationship asks first or loudest. If we did, we would throw our lives into chaos. Unfortunately, the truth of priority decision-making is not being taught to most people. So people feel they must just live faster to get it all done, or they neglect crucial relationships that are not loud or insistent.

Let me help you see the principle of prioritized relationships. When I go to the mailbox, I receive appeals to send money to worthwhile causes. If I gave to each of these requests, I wouldn't have any money left to pay my house payment, feed my family, tithe to my church, enjoy hobbies, or grow as an individual. Therefore, my money cannot be given out based upon what comes in my mailbox. I must have a structure or order that tells me who to give my money to and how much I should give. Usually, that means we pay the government first (usually because the government takes it out before we see it). Then we give to our church. We pay our bills. Then we see how much we have left over for fun and recreation. It is only after these basics are covered that we can look at giving to other groups. If you have no structure and you spend your money on whatever you feel like until it's gone, you'll soon be in a terrible mess or on the street.

In the same way, we must establish a priority structure across the ten major relationships of our lives. Each of these relationships requires a certain amount of time, energy, and money to be healthy and contribute positively to our lives. No one of these relationships is capable of supplying all we need for life to be meaningful, significant, and fulfilling. Even God in perfect relationship with Adam said, "It is not good for man to be alone." Our time, energy, and resources must be divided up and distributed to each of these relationships in a manner where they will thrive.

Each relationship can push its way to dominance and create havoc in life. Here are some examples in each of the nine major relationships other than marriage to understand why you must have a priority structure for your relationships.

God

I remember a woman who was so enamored with her personal relationship with God that she began praying 10-12 hours a day. There is nothing wrong with prayer, but this woman had young children and a husband. Spending that much time in prayer put her marriage and family into crisis. It can't be God's will to neglect your duty to other relationships to focus on Him. In fact, that is why the apostle Paul suggests it would be better to stay single, if you can, to devote more time to God (1 Cor. 7:7-9, 32). If you have a family, you must be a functional, responsible caretaker of it. Even Jesus, while dying on the cross, made arrangements for His mother to be taken care of (John 19:26, 27).

Personal Development

I have watched people spend 6-8 hours each day exercising, devoting every waking moment to school, spending 4-5 days a week playing golf, or spending every spare minute working on their favorite hobby. This unlimited time on self radically affects other relationships. Those pursuits are good things, but spending that much time on them is not good.

Marriage

This entire book is about strengthening and/or saving marriages, and it is important to emphasize that husbands and wives must provide a minimum of one to two hours every day—and more on one's days off—to minister to the needs of their spouse and to be ministered to by their partner. If the relational needs that are a part of our marriage are not met, it is inevitable that the marriage will shrivel and eventually become a mere business relationship or die altogether.

When our marriage relationship has been neglected for a long time, we should spend more time on that relationship. If a marriage has been strained, I recommend that a couple spend at least two hours a day ministering to each other's relational needs. If the relationship is near separation or divorce, take a few days or a week away from work and the kids when all you do is have fun with each other.

Just like any garden or houseplant, a certain amount of time, energy, and resources is needed to keep the marriage relationship alive and healthy. Remember that your spouse's relational needs are rarely yours, so it will take some sacrifice and effort on your part to meet your spouse's needs. But it will be worth it. To make sure your marriage survives and thrives, plug it into your schedule every day to meet your spouse's needs.

Family

I have seen people spend every waking moment thinking about, caring for, and being with their children, leaving no time for their spouse, personal development, or relationship with God. I have also watched men and women neglect their marriage to devote huge amounts of time to parents or in-laws. Many people excuse this kind of imbalance because it is family. Certainly there are seasons when more time must be devoted because of a tragedy or special circumstances; but after the crisis is over, your time, energy, and resource allotment must return to normal priority structures or other relationships will begin to suffer. I have often seen a marriage die because a temporary problem is allowed to go on for five, ten, and, in some cases, twenty years with no change in time or energy allotments.

"My mother needs me."

"My brother needs me."

"We must do this for the children."

Work

I work with couples who are considering separation and divorce because one of them spends so much time at work that the marriage is neglected. One of the most common complaints of wives is that their husbands spend all their time at work, often 50-70 hours a week. The man justifies this because he is providing for his family. But if he gives his family money but no time or energy, he has not truly provided for his family's needs.

Church

Surprisingly, it is possible for the church to ask for too much time and energy. I have seen men and women become so involved in their church that they spend four to six nights a week in church activity, neglecting their spouse and family. That is unhealthy. It is wonderful to be committed to God's work; but your marriage, family, work, and community involvements are also God's work. These other relationships need you to be healthy and functioning properly in them as well.

Finances/Money Management

Very few people have a good handle on healthy money management. Most of us are tempted to spend money impulsively or foolishly or go into debt. The strain of these decisions impacts marriage. Advertisers want us to spend every last cent on their products. They don't care if we don't have enough for other things; they just want us to purchase their products. It takes time and knowledge to ensure that the financial aspects of our lives work. If we do not invest time, we live in the chaos that our lack of planning creates. I have seen marriages torn apart because one partner was consumed with money. The imbalance can destroy the relationship. In fact, the number one reason cited for divorce in America is financial difficulties.

Society/Community

I have watched people so consumed with good causes in their community—a political campaign or little league—that they neglect everything else. It is not wrong to get involved in worthy causes. In fact, it is noble and needed. But we cannot allow good things in our society to destroy foundational relationships in our lives. It is often too late when the husband or wife realizes that he or she has put so much into the good societal thing that their marriage has been destroyed. After the divorce, all that's left is a feeling of hollowness.

Friends

I have actually seen husbands and wives spend so much time with their friends that they essentially squeeze their spouse right out of their lives. I saw one lady develop a friendship with a woman at work that became obsessive. Whatever the friend wanted to do was what needed to be done, even when it involved going to bars and picking up men. This friendship eventually destroyed her marriage and her relationship with her children. Of course, after the marriage was destroyed, the friend disappeared also. I have seen people spend time with the wrong friends and end up in drug abuse and alcoholism. If a friend is destroying your marriage, he or she is not really your friend.

Enemies

I have seen men and women build their lives around seeking revenge on their enemies. There are people who definitely deserve some form of justice, but a focus on revenge consumes and destroys. Everyone has been wounded or hurt—some in particularly awful ways. Sometimes it's a father who was abusive. It could be an ex-partner in business who was a cheat. Sometimes it is an ex-marriage partner who bad-mouthed and stole from the former spouse. Sometimes it is a current boss or an irritating neighbor. We all have enemies, but if we allow them to define what we think much of the time, it's unhealthy. Don't let your opponents define your thoughts. Seek justice. Learn how to forgive and rebuild your life. You have nine other relationships that need your attention—don't let one or two bad apples spoil everything else.

As you can see from these examples, life must have structure to provide nurture and attention to all our relationships. We can't afford to be fixated on any one relationship to the point that it throws the rest out of balance.

There are great resources at any local church and/or Christian counseling center to help one work through an overemphasis on one of the ten major relationships. Often your spouse can tell if you are spending too much time on another relationship. Listen, even if you don't like what you are hearing. The amount of time and energy you spend may seem okay to you, but it may be threatening your marriage relationship. Don't be the last to know—ask.

Marriage Solutions and Exercises

Take a Relationship Review. Ask yourself, your spouse, or a trusted friend to answer the following questions about you.

- How is my work/life balance?
- Are there any aspects of my life in which I am overcommitted?
- How am I unbalanced: time, energy, or money?
- What does the right balance look like to you?
- How much time do you perceive me spending in each of these areas each week?
  - o God
  - o Self
  - o Marriage
  - o Family
  - o Work
  - o Church
  - o Money
  - o Society
  - o Friends
  - o Enemies

The Big Three

The three most common areas that damage a marriage by overcommitment are finances, work, and family. One of these areas may dominate one or both partners in dysfunctional ways until it drains the life and joy out of a marriage. It is not until discipline, reason, and boundaries are added that the marriage has any chance of recovery. In the next section we will spend time on an appropriate priority structure and a biblical pattern of success for each of the "big three."

Finances

Most Americans have had little or no training on strategies to make their finances work to their advantage. Therefore, a marriage may have two ill-prepared people ignoring the financial arena of their lives, hoping there will be enough money to meet their needs and dreams. There never is enough money for both people. In fact, in a consumer-oriented world, advertisers do all they can to make sure you never have enough money for all they have induced you to want. The number one reason cited for divorce in the United States is money. That means that two people can't agree on how to handle their money. Both sides believe their way of managing and spending money is the best way and neither side wants to give in. It usually results in a disastrous financial picture with both parties spending the same money. In essence, the money is spent twice.

There is a need for basic financial intelligence. What are the fundamental principles required to have a positive and healthy relationship with money? Jesus referred to money as the only inanimate thing with which we have a relationship (Matt. 6:24). The question is whether it will be healthy or unhealthy. A healthy relationship with money doesn't depend upon how much you have; it is far more complex than that.

Handling money well requires time and planning. Every person must learn those key principles of handling money with wisdom. There are great resources available to gain wisdom in the financial arena of life. Dave Ramsey's material, *Financial Peace University*, is a good resource.[1] Crown Financial Ministries is another great resource.[2] Ron Blue is a well-known speaker, writer, and teacher on helpful financial management principles.[3] The Willow Creek Association also has great financial teaching resources called, "Good Sense."[4] These and many other experts go into much more depth than I can in this small section on finances.

You have a relationship with money. You have patterns and feelings about money that determine where you are financially. If your parents or someone else did not teach you how to handle money well, then you are at the mercy of advertisers and peddlers. Many couples can't talk calmly and rationally about money. They ignore the subject until there is too little money left at the end of the month and then they fight about who spent what. You must know how money works and the rules to having enough of it, so you can talk calmly and rationally with your partner. If one or both parties are violating basic principles of finances, you must discuss it and come up with a solution.

To keep your finances from draining your marriage, you must bring a proper understanding and balance between three basic elements of the financial arena: income, management, and giving. All financial plans work with these elements. The following are the basic principles and solutions in each of the three areas, so your marriage can return to health.

Income

A marriage requires a certain amount of income to survive and more to thrive. You can't live on love alone. Different marriages require different amounts, but income is always required. I have worked with couples who want a great marriage, but they don't want to work hard to bring in money. If a husband doesn't work, it is virtually impossible to make the marriage work. His supply of income to the family is crucial. If he has a thousand excuses for why it's not the right time, job, or situation, his marriage will be in trouble. Even if he is injured, he is still responsible for making sure the proper amount of income flows into the marriage. I remember working with a man who was declared disabled because of injuries he had sustained. No one would hire him in his chosen field, so he found something his body could do and started his own business to provide for his family.

It is very popular these days for both husbands and wives to work full time to afford the lifestyle they want. Be very careful about both people working to the end of their energy and time to make financial issues work. I have seen people buy too big a house with no room to breathe financially. One of the two individuals falters under the workload, and then the financial house of cards begins to fall apart. When you build your financial plan, always leave about 30 percent of your income flexible. You will need room for the unexpected.

Marriage Solutions and Exercises

Take a financial income review. Ask yourself the following questions.

- How much income do we have?
- How could we make more income?

- Do we have any forms of passive income? (Passive income is money you receive from any source you did not work to earn. It could include investments, rental income, royalties from intellectual property or books, or a business you own but do not operate, etc.)

- Could we create passive forms of income?

- Should we go back to school or seek more training?

- What area of interest remains unexplored as a potential income source?

- Are we saving enough money so that one day we won't have to work? Will we be able someday to live off the interest of our savings?

- How will we increase our salary? This usually requires new skills, new opportunities, promotions, and/or schooling.

- Are we willing to explore new opportunities? (I have watched missed opportunities come and go for those unwilling to take a risk.)

- What new opportunities are coming our way? How should we check them out?

- What changes can we make to our financial plan or money management that will bring in or save our family $10,000-15,000 more next year?

Management

The second area of smart financial thinking is management. In the western world most couples make enough money, but they don't manage it very well. Most people follow a disastrous plan called Management by Desire. "I will spend money only on what I really want." That type of spending plan will never work. Our desire can't be the deciding factor for how we spend money.

The key insight in the management of money is to tell your money where you want it to go rather than allowing others to dictate it for you. Almost everyone has a plan for your money—your children, parents, friends, charities, storeowners, and advertisers. But the only people who can make your finances work are the two of you. Those other people will not say they are trying to control your money, but they will want you to buy a new toy, go on a trip with them, donate toward a great cause, or buy their product, even if you can't afford it.

You have to sit down at the beginning of each month and/or year and write out a plan for where you want your money to go. Then you have to follow your money plan. This is usually called a budget, but that word is so emotionally negative to most people that I call it a money plan. Your money is impulsive, like a little puppy. It is your money plan that trains it and directs it how to act. You can spend your money on whatever you want, but only a few things will cause your finances to work long-term. We must take the time to think about what is really important and what we want to accomplish with our money. It is beneficial for both husband and wife to work through the process of what they want to do with their money.

A basic percentages formula is the best way to get a handle on your money. Financial experts have worked out basic percentages that are required for each area of life. Obviously, the numbers given are subject to change for different situations and contexts, but these percentages give couples a helpful starting place. Too many couples want to make a wish list instead of a money plan. Remember, you cannot spend more than 100 percent of your money. The following is a basic money plan.

Category	Percentage	Actual Monthly Amount	Actual Yearly Amount
Tithe	10%		
Housing	39%		
Food	12%		

Auto	12%		
Debts	5%		
Entertainment/ Recreation	6%		
Clothing	5%		
Savings	5%		
Miscellaneous	6%		
Total	100%		

You must adjust different categories lower or higher to meet your specific needs so no more than 100 percent is spent. There may be other categories specific to your family that need to be added. The use of these percentages at the beginning is a very good way to start. Make sure that what you spend is within the acceptable range for your income.

Typical Budget Busters

There are usually three spending areas that destroy our budgets: housing (including utilities), recreation/entertainment, and debt. Many financial counselors will tell a couple if they're spending more than 40 percent on their house (unless they make more than $150,000 per year), they will not make it financially. Something must change. Here are a few options: start earning more money, find a lower interest rate, lower your utilities drastically, or purchase a smaller house. If you are spending more than 15 percent on recreation/entertainment (unless you are in the upper income brackets), you won't make it.

Many times it is going out to eat, maintaining a boat, owning a timeshare, or involvement in hobbies and sports teams that is busting the budget. Those activities need to be brought into alignment with the reality of what you make, not what you desire. We might wish we had unlimited money to get what we want, go where we want, and do what we want, but we usually have only six percent of our net income to use in this area. That is not very much. If a couple makes

$3,000 a month, six percent is $180 a month or $45 per week. Most couples find if management is the problem in their finances, they have to go to some kind of envelope system. Put in the amount you can spend in that category each week. When the envelope is empty, you can't do anything else.

The third budget buster is debt. If your debt load reaches more than 15 percent, it is another strong indicator you will not make it financially. Credit cards, loans, get-rich schemes, and shaky investments are promoted everywhere in this society. Most couples need to get rid of their credit cards and use only debit cards and checks to overcome this problem. Usually, the best way to pay back debt is the snowball plan. Pay as much extra as you can on one bill until it is paid off and then add this amount to the next smallest bill. Each bill that is paid off adds more money to the next largest bill. This plan works and progress is made against debt.

If you and your spouse are willing to face reality in these three areas, your money plan can work. Your finances are where they are because you have the financial habits you do. You need to add some new habits and get rid of old habits. Do not lie to yourself that somehow if you keep doing the same things with your money, you will get a different result. Don't let money be the reason you don't have a good marriage. Your growth into a new level of financial health may take time and coaching, but it's worth it.

Marriage Solutions and Exercises

- Keep track of everything you spend for one month.

- Plug the amounts into the percentages formula. You may find you need to shift money around. You may find the percentages won't work because of your house payment or some other fixed cost. That is common, and you need to think through what that means long-term for the financial and emotional health of your marriage. I have watched too many people divorce because they couldn't emotionally sell the house or part with their favorite car. Eventually, they lose everything in the divorce and much more. The most important thing is your marriage, not the material things you have accumulated. Get the marriage healthy, and you can get all that stuff back; but if you lose the marriage, it is almost always financial suicide.

- Write down what you make every month from all sources.

- Based upon your income number, figure out the percentages in each category.

- Use or develop an envelope system that tells you when to stop spending in a category.

- Write down what you would like to buy this next year. This is a wish list of purchases, vacations, clothing, etc. Both husband and wife should make a list and then look at each other's lists. Then the two lists should undergo lots of discussion and be combined into a prioritized list. If there is excess money, decide what to do first. If you do not stick to the prioritized list, the allure of advertisers, sales, and deals will make you resent your spouse because you can't buy what you want.

- Why do you need to make this list? It is better to get your desires out in the open and have a rational discussion than resent the other person for holding you back. If both parties don't have anything to look forward to until the kids leave, it doesn't make for a great marriage.

Work/Career

There is something alluring and demanding about being needed at work. The company needs me. This project can't survive without my involvement. There will always be more projects, deals, and promotions to tackle than time in the day. If we're not careful, we will be completely sucked into our work environment and slowly lose the love and joy of our marriages. To maintain a good marriage, spend at least an hour a day of quality interaction with your spouse. It is best if you give your marriage between two-four hours each day or one-third of your day for your family. Both partners want to have an attentive spouse who can disengage from work. More and more couples find they think about work all the time and resent their spouse's demands to think about something else. People are being tempted into affairs at work because this continues the work focus. Discussions in the affair are about topics the person finds interesting and compelling. Do not destroy your marriage and family over a career that is only one piece of a full life.

Ask yourself these questions:

- How much time should be devoted to work, including my commute?

- How much of my focus should be upon my career?

- Should my marriage and family life be subservient to maximizing a career?

- What is the right work/life balance?

These types of questions often flow from a man's desire to make a name for himself. But more people of both genders are asking these questions.

I can remember saying to one couple, "I can't fix your marriage until you (the husband) either change jobs or move within 15 minutes of where you work." I had tried everything with the couple and nothing worked. His daily hour-and-a-half commute each way meant there was not enough time and energy left when he got home. Thankfully, they took my advice, sold their home, and moved within five minutes of his work. They gained three hours each day to minister to each other, relax, indulge in hobbies, and become well-rounded people.

Ask yourself, if you had only this job, would life be full and complete? I think the answer for everyone is *no*. The only time the answer feels like a yes is in our late twenties and early thirties, but even then we need the relationships we have at work. It takes all ten relationships to build a full life. God has designed us so we have not one, but ten relationships to feed love, care, and joy into our lives. Our present culture tells us if you find something you like, put all your eggs in that basket. That is a very risky and foolhardy strategy. To really have balance, joy, and peace during the good times and the bad, we must have more than just work. A full life requires God, a healthy self-concept, a loving marriage and family, interesting and important work, a church where spiritual growth and deep relationships are possible, a healthy financial picture, a functioning community, good friends, and some level of peace with our enemies.

How do you bring balance to work? It usually begins with boundaries. It is important to set maximums for the amount of work you do each day and week. Schedule how to spend your time. Schedule time to focus on your marriage and family. Schedule time for exercise and friends. Schedule time for church and personal time with God. Do not let the squeaky wheel of work always win. When you are home, you should be at home mentally. If you operate a home-based business, designate times not to answer the phones, look at e-mails, or respond to faxes.

I worked with one couple trying to repair their marriage. The man's work would demand overtime almost every weekend. The boss was divorced, so he had nothing better to do than be at the office. It was always spur of the moment. "Charlie, something has come up this weekend. We need you to work Saturday and Sunday mornings." That happened three out of four weekends every month. When we identified this as a major relational drain on his marriage, we worked out a plan. Charlie was to go into work on Monday and tell his boss the overtime was damaging his marriage and family. He loved working there but couldn't do the overtime every weekend. He was willing to work 48 hours during the normal week, which included eight hours of overtime each week, but he was not going to work most weekends anymore. Charlie was willing to work one weekend a month but no more. The boss had heard this speech before and expected Charlie to give in once he learned what was needed. But the next weekend, Charlie had a priority structure. He told his boss politely he wasn't coming. He couldn't be away from his wife and children anymore. This was the beginning of a whole new respect for Charlie. His boss later confided this was why his own marriage had broken up.

A creative way many people are dealing with the work/life balance issue is to include their family in their business trips. The inclusion of your family in your career makes you a team. Whatever you do, you must not allow your work to become your whole life. Even people who are always on call must learn how to go on dates and family outings while on call. It may require a new level of creativity, but make it work.

Marriage Solutions and Exercises

- If you have had a stressful week at work, take time off to be with your spouse and/or family.

- Honestly evaluate if your current work/life balance works.

- Answer the following questions and be willing to make changes if necessary:

  o What is the maximum amount of time I give to my work on a regular basis?

    45 hours a week   50 hours a week
    55 hours a week   60 hours a week
    65 hours a week   70 hours a week

  o Is my spouse in agreement that our marriage will not suffer because of this time?

  o When is the best time to give one to four hours to my spouse and family? (Go through each day and block out time. Make sure your spouse agrees.)

    Monday:
    Tuesday:
    Wednesday:
    Thursday:
    Friday:
    Saturday:
    Sunday:

  o Is it possible for me to have adequate marriage and family time in my present job?
    * Husband:
    * Wife:

  o Can I have a healthy marriage with this job?

  o What changes could I make to increase my marital health?

o Are there other available jobs that would increase my marital health?

o What other career fields could increase my marital health?

o With some jobs there are also problems of pressure, stress, and trauma. Those jobs don't leave enough emotional energy for marriage and family. One has the time but no emotional energy because of what the job does to him or her. Does that describe me?

Family/ Children

One of the unforeseen dangers to some marriages is the very thing a good marriage often produces—children. It is easy to shift the focus onto the children so that little time is left for keeping the marriage healthy. It seems like such a noble thing, but it can be a relationship killer if there's not enough time given to each other as well as to the children. When children come, they need constant time and attention; and if you're not careful, there is little time for the two of you. Usually, the wife is the most tempted to spend all her time and energy on the children. It is important to make sure the children have all they need to grow to become healthy adults, but if focusing on them excludes your spouse and his needs, it is destructive.

Whatever else was to take place in life, you pledged your energy and attention to meet your spouse's relational needs and vice versa. When other things crowd out time to listen, date, romance, admire each other, do hobbies together, or experience sexual intimacy, then those things become the enemies of your marriage. Unfortunately, children in some homes are allowed to become the number one enemy of the marriage. The usual ways are: first, unlimited amount of time, attention, and focus on the children; second, disagreements on how to raise the children; and third, a child-dominated home.

Enjoying Your Children

The issue that often divides husbands and wives is how to raise children to become responsible and enjoyable. One parent is almost always more strict than the other. Children can exploit this natural split in many homes and cause chaos. You need to have a plan for raising your children and living to tell about it. Children are wonderful additions to any home, but you must follow certain basic rules to parent well-adjusted children. If your children are terrors or lazy, no one will enjoy them—including you.

There are four elements all great families have in common: *respect, responsibility, rules, and relationship*. If these four pillars are embedded in you and your children, you will raise great kids and have a great time in the process. Children who can control their minds and body to be productive and appropriately relational are enjoyable children. Children who obey whatever impulse pops into their mind or body are not enjoyable. Children who serve only themselves and do not help produce loving relationships are not enjoyable.

This is not a handbook for parenting, but I have included a few key ideas and exercises that will unite husband and wife to solve the mystery of child rearing. I highly recommend Steve Sherbondy's "*Changing Your Child's Heart*"[5] as an excellent resource. What follows are basic parenting principles that serve as a foundation for a great and enjoyable family. They are arranged under the headings of the four keys to great parenting mentioned earlier. More could be said than the few actions outlined in this short overview, but this will help a couple start parenting on a good foundation.

Respect

Never disagree with the other parent in front of the children. If children realize they can play the parents against each another, they will often take advantage. Successful parents discuss disagreements in private not in public. If your spouse allows something you would handle differently, suggest a private discussion on the matter. Do not enter a debate in front of the children. Only in the case of significant physical or psychological damage should open disagreements between parents be allowed. There will be disagreements between parents on what to allow and restrict, but this heated interaction must take place in private, so you make a unified front before the children. If you are not unified, then a decision has not been reached, and you should tell the children you are still discussing it.

Require the use of proper titles. This doesn't seem like a big deal today with its easy familiarity, but it is crucial that children recognize a line of respect between themselves and adults. This means that children should not call their parents by their first names. They should refer to them as Mother, Father, Dad, Mom, or other affectionate and respectful terms. If your children refer to you by your first names, the habit should be corrected. Remind your kids that there are only a few people in the world who call you Dad and Mom, and they are the ones.

Children should not call other adults by their first names either, even if the adult wants them to. We found inserting a Mr. or Ms. in front of the first name of a person who wanted to be called by their first name was sufficient to create the level of respect necessary. Without these customs of respect, children get the idea that they are equal in authority to adults, so they don't need to conform their behavior or speech to anyone else. They are the gods of their own world. If children grow up thinking they are equal in authority to everyone else, as teens they will think they can do anything they want. There will be one fewer check against rebellious independence. Proper titles and respectful use of names are subtle but constant reminders of the differences between an adult and a child.

Now let me say you *do* want your children to grow into independence. You want them to make more and more responsible decisions as they incorporate themselves into the real world. If they believe they are gods and don't have to listen to anyone, they will be slammed by the real world. It will be a rude awakening.

Rules

Stabilize their world through bedtime, meal times, wake-up time, chores, and routine. Do not allow your children to follow their impulses when they go to bed, when they eat, when they wake up, what chores they do, and the routines they follow. If you allow them to be impulse-driven in those basic areas, they will learn their impulses are king and should be obeyed. As they grow older, that idea is disastrous. There is an idea we should allow our children to fall asleep when they want to and to stay up as long as they want at very young ages. That allows their inward impulses to be king, meaning one moment they could be great and at other times they could be complete terrors. And it's all based upon whether they feel like it or not. If you are going to raise enjoyable children, you must help them realize that they can't act on their inward impulses. Regulating these basic behaviors wins a subtle war with your children's selfish impulses. Giving your children significant amounts of routine causes them to experience the trumping of internal impulses by relational needs. This is crucial to an enjoyable family life.

They live inside your box. Help your children understand they live inside the box (limits) you set for their safety and maximum development. The box gets bigger or smaller by their choices, actions, and attitudes. The box is small when they are young and grows bigger as they demonstrate maturity. It doesn't automatically get larger as they get older. When they go outside the box with their actions or speech, you may have to discipline them. They must not believe you are arbitrary or capricious, punishing them for unknown reasons. They must know as long as they stay inside of a consistent set of boundaries, everything is okay in their world.

The three-day rule. If you stand firm on a rule, chore, or action for three days, your children will give in and adjust their world to accommodate the new rule. You can't waver or change during the three days. Your children will do everything to get you to fail to implement the rule; but if you stay firm, three days later there will be peace. I overheard one of my daughters say to her younger sister, "You might as well give in; Dad won't change his mind. I have tried everything—I mean everything—and he doesn't change once he's made up his mind." You can't give in, or you shouldn't have made the rule in the first place. It may be a battle for three days as they bring out all the techniques they have seen work in the past. If you are observant, you can see their whole arsenal of tricks to get you to give in. Most children will adjust and adapt before three days, but the strong-willed ones will take the whole three days. Eventually, they will realize this is the new reality.

Action, not anger. All children test the boundaries their parents have set for them. They want to know where the fences are. They need some kind of response from you to signify they have reached the edge of your boundary. Too many parents think that setting the boundaries will cause the children to respect those boundaries forever. It doesn't work that way. Your children will continue to probe and push until they get a reaction from you, so they will know there really is a boundary. If there is no reaction, it wasn't a boundary to begin with.

What most parents do is wait until they are angry enough to retaliate against the child in some way. This is damaging in a number of ways. First, it causes the child to think the boundary is further out than it really is. Second, it teaches your children that you are always angry with them when they push against the boundary. Third, it teaches them you will not do anything until you get angry. Wherever you put a boundary, you must be willing to act in some way to support it. If you want your children home at a certain time, enforce it. If you want them to stop hitting their brother, enforce it with action. If you want them to brush their teeth, take action.

It is possible and preferable for you to move the action line and the anger line quite far apart. You can decide to take action in response to something at any point you want. You do not have to wait until you are so annoyed or frustrated you can't sit still anymore. It is best to note the activities and actions of your children that make you angry or irritated and determine you will take action way before your children get to that point. You don't have to be dramatic or forceful in your actions. Any type of action that derails the trajectory of their behavior will do. Don't wait until you're angry. Act early.

Responsibility

Make the expectations clear. Don't think, "They know how they should act." Spell it out to them again. Spell it out before the possible difficulty. Here is a suggested way of communicating proper behavior before you go to Grandma's house.

When we go into Grandma's house, here is how I want you to act and react for the next two hours. Grandma always offers cookies near the end of the visit, not at the beginning. Wait until she offers. Grandma will tell many of the same stories over again. You need to listen and act interested. You are allowed to go to the bathroom only three times while we are at Grandma's. And don't play with the statues in her bathroom.

Directions like that need to be repeated over and over again, so the children clearly understand what is expected of them. Realize that they may not remember how to behave. Remind them what positive behavior looks like.

My wife and I found that every time we went out to eat (especially when the children were little), it went much better if I stopped the children before we went into the restaurant and explained the blow-by-blow description of how we wanted them to act in the restaurant. I would kneel down and tell the children exactly how we expected them to behave. We described in detail the positive behaviors we wanted them to do in as close to chronological order as possible. Our children want to please us, but they often are not clearly reminded right before the new situation, so they forget and let their impulses get the best of them. Be positive, not negative. Tell them what you want them to do instead of what not to do. Some negatives will come up but be more positive.

Understand basic positive and negative training methods and goals. Training your children to become responsible citizens and God-honoring people requires both positive and negative methods. They surprisingly boil down to just a few basic ways. Some ways fit your personality and some don't. There may be times when you need to use techniques and training methods that are new to you. But the key question is always, "What will make my children realize their responsibility and make the right choice next time?" Another question to ask yourself is, "Am I causing a changed heart attitude and behavior in my children?" If the answer is no, then it clearly isn't working with them. You need to change to a different way of interacting with your children. Do not repeat the same forms of discipline, correction, or punishment if they aren't producing better behavior. Realize what you're doing isn't working and switch to a different method.

Verbal reminder and rebuke. Some children are so sensitive that a simple reminder is all they need. If a verbal rebuke or look of disappointment will cause them not to repeat the behavior, there is no need to do anything more.

Rewards for right behavior. Some children respond best when they achieve something for the desired behavior. It could be a treat or desired item, but the desire for the reward provides sufficient incentive to behave. This technique is used often in the learning of a new behavior like potty training or learning multiplication tables.

Removal of privileges. Some children are very motivated to change when specific privileges are threatened. They value privileges such as the telephone, TV, friends, and youth group; and they are willing to act differently so those privileges will continue. This is not about punishing your children; it is about changing their behavior. It doesn't matter if you want to take away privileges because you're angry. It only matters whether it will bring about a new set of behaviors in your children.

Moral reasoning: the five questions. At times it is helpful to have a moral reasoning conversation with your child about wrong behavior. In this conversation, you will ask them five questions they must answer. Here are the questions:

- "What did you do?"
- "Was that the right or wrong behavior in the situation?"
- "What could you have done other than what you did?"
- "What do we need to do so you won't forget to make a different choice next time?"
- "What will you choose next time?"

Whatever was decided in the fourth question needs to be administered. That helps your child understand they do have a choice, and they don't have to follow their impulses. It takes time and should be done in private.

Restraint. There are times when children might hurt themselves by dashing out into traffic, touching a hot stove, or breaking sharp objects. In these kinds of situations, it may be appropriate to restrain the child for a period of time until order is restored or the unsafe situation has passed.

Restate expectations. Sometimes it is sufficient to restate the expectations and have the child repeat them. This practice alone produces the sufficient amount of learning so negative behavior will not recur. Ask the child what he or she was supposed to do in the situation rather than what he or she did. Making the child restate the expectations three times may be sufficient for the proper correction of behavior. If the behavior changes, no further correction is needed.

Practice. One of the most helpful but overlooked training techniques for misdeeds is having the child do it correctly three to five times in a row. If they came through the door slamming it as they entered, then they need to practice coming through the door the right way. Requiring them to come through the door quietly and respectfully three to five times is often sufficient to remind the child not to slam the door again. I have found this technique so clarifying for children. They really do need to practice doing something right so they can get praise for it. When children realize their parents will make them practice doing something the right way, they conclude it's not worth doing the convenient, but wrong, thing.

Isolation. Our world has gone overboard on time-outs for children who misbehave, but there are situations when time-outs are appropriate ways to change behavior in the child. Isolation is not the panacea many people think it is, but it can be an effective tool for training. If the child's behavior changes because they have had a time-out, it was the right technique; but if the child continues the behavior, then time-out or being sent to his or her room is not the right technique.

Work. There are times when a child's attitude is out of sorts, and he or she needs to work it out. In these cases, a slow and mindless task can help him or her to work through the issues. I have known parents who have told their children, "Your attitude is not right. I think you need some time to change it, so I want you to vacuum the whole house." Other chores like that could be to sweep out the garage, clean the tiles in the shower, shovel the snow in the driveway, or dust the furniture. The key idea is when your attitude is different and the chore is done, it is over. If the attitude is the same (surly and rebellious), the chores keep coming. This kind of mindless chore usually gives children time to think and realize they need a change of attitude.

Exercises. There are times when chores and work will not change the child's attitude. In those instances some parents have used push-ups, pull-ups, sit-ups, and jumping jacks. The child needs to work out this level of aggression and rebellion. He or she needs to understand that that kind of attitude and behavior will not be tolerated. This is essentially a military training technique without the drill instructor shouting insulting remarks. It is an effective method for helping your children realize they can change their attitude and behavior any time they want to. If they don't, it will be unpleasant for them. This is often needed for the strong-willed child. Something inside the child says, "Do not submit to what others want, even if you know it is right."

Corporal punishment. There are times of direct defiance and rebellion when corporal punishment is needed to emphasize that the behavior will not be tolerated. Care must be taken to ensure the use of corporal punishment will not result in injury. It is also important to note the amount of corporal punishment should not exceed the level of open love and affection for the child. It is naive to believe every child will respond to discussions and time-outs. There are times when a child basically says to his or her parents "Make me!" It is at those times that corporal punishment may be appropriate.

Whatever form of training is used, the goal is to have your children become responsible for their actions, words, attitudes, and motives. Children who understand that they are responsible for their attitudes, actions, words, thoughts, and motives will be successful in life.

Relationship

Eat at least four to five meals a week together for discussion, devotions, and fun. Columbia University did a study in which they noted 12 different activities families could do that would guarantee children would not take drugs as they grew older.[6] One of those activities was eating at least four to five dinner meals together per week. Make sure there is adequate family time around something pleasant. Be encouraging to one another around the dinner table. Ask about the day and how things went. Be genuinely interested in their concerns and issues. The family meal should not be a time to consume food quickly but should instead be a place for conversation, concern, love, and attention.

Remove the television and computer from the bedrooms of your children and put them in a common area. The proverb says, "He who separates himself argues against all sound wisdom" (see Proverbs 18:1). Your children will naturally want to isolate themselves from you as they grow older and build a new mental paradigm where their ideas are agreed with and supported. However, they need to live in the real world that includes your interests, respectful interaction, and regular supervision. One of the ways children like to isolate themselves is through television, phones, computers, and music. We have found if children have to come out into the common area of the home to view television or to work on the computer, it forces them to interact with the family and the real world. Children who have all the technology in their rooms can become distant from their family. Having private space is a wonderful thing, but too much private space can allow them to be selfish and sullen. They can learn a lot and correct a lot as they are forced to defer to others in the family. This is an essential socialization and maturation exercise. It may be initially easier to let them be in their room, but it will not be easier later.

Do fun things as a family weekly, quarterly, and yearly. Go on dates with your children and do fun activities together, so there is a huge pile of good memories your children have of hanging out with you and their siblings. Take regular vacations with interesting things to do and see. Make sure you take lots of pictures of them having fun and enjoying their siblings. Without the pictures, they can convince themselves your family is boring, never does anything fun, and really doesn't care about them. It will take planning and money, but it is well worth it. Ask your spouse and your kids what family vacations they want to take this year. Their answers will surprise you. Visit all the local museums and tourist attractions within five hours of your home. Parenting an enjoyable family is hard work, but it is one of the most rewarding experiences you can have.

Let your children talk without interruption or correction. As your children grow up, they need to be able to express themselves to you. At times what they say may be wrong or inaccurate, but it is important you listen with rapt attention. Let them get it all out before you correct the inaccuracies. Talking is how we communicate who we are, and listening is the way people let us know they love us. If children are not able to express themselves without interruption and correction, they conclude their parents are not safe people to talk to. This is especially true in the teen years. If you want to be a part of their world as they grow toward independence, you must listen as they work through various ideas and thoughts. When the children are in their teen years, stop making statements and start asking questions.

Make sure children get more respect, praise, and appreciation from you than anyone else. We are like flowers turning toward the sun. We naturally move in the direction of those who respect, praise, and encourage us. Your children are no different. They will view as friends people who overlook their flaws and trumpet their strengths and victories. If the people who celebrate them are immoral people, your child will be drawn towards an immoral lifestyle. We need people to praise us, cheer for us, and value us. We will automatically move toward whoever values us the most. It is important that the most praise, encouragement, and value come from you, or they will move away from you and toward whoever provides it. It's very easy in the parenting process to keep pointing to your children's failings, weaknesses, and difficulties. While it is important to help children grow to maturity, correct mistakes, and be well rounded, it is more important that they be celebrated for their unique contributions, talents, and strengths.

Parents unconsciously determine how close their children are to them by the level of appreciation, praise, and encouragement they give them. If you want to start drawing your children to you, make sure they receive more praise and encouragement from you than anyone else in their lives.

Marriage Solutions and Exercises

- Make time to focus on your spouse every day. It is best if it is the same time every day so it becomes routine. Make it a mutual expectation.

- When is your designated time to spend with your spouse? You must schedule time as life gets busier and busier. There are so many people pulling at you. If you are not disciplined, the most important person in your life will get little of your time. If you let that happen, you will allow your marriage to slip into a business relationship. Take the basic weekly chart below and schedule when you will spend time with your spouse.

Mon	Tues	Wed	Thurs	Fri	Sat	Sun

- Have a discussion with your spouse about each of your children and which "R" they need to work on this week. It might change from week to week.

- Work only on the specific "R" the child needs most. Work on the other stuff later. You can't work on it all at once. Start somewhere and make progress in that arena. Then agree together when it is time to switch to another issue.

- Make two or three 3x5 cards, listing the specific actions listed under "respect" and put them on the refrigerator. Carry one with you as well. If you are working on respect with one of your children, remind yourself of those ways before you work with them.

- Make two or three 3x5 cards, noting the specific actions listed under "rules" and put them on the refrigerator. Carry one with you as well. If you are working on rules with one of your children, remind yourself of those ways before you work with them.

- Make two or three 3x5 cards, noting the specific actions listed under "responsibility" and put them on the refrigerator. Carry one with you as well. If you are working on responsibility with one of your children, remind yourself of those ways before you work with them.

- Make two or three 3x5 cards of the specific actions listed under "relationship" and put them on the refrigerator. Carry one with you as well. If you are working on relationship with one of your children, remind yourself of those ways before you work with them.

Summary of the Problem of Competing Relationships

If there is not an intentional focus on your marriage with dedicated time for husband and wife every day, the marriage vitality will begin to drain away. There are ten major relationships in life, and all must be kept in a balanced priority structure.

Most couples during courtship and the early part of marriage focus on each other adequately. What many couples don't think about is the pull of other relationships in life that clamor and rip away time and energy from the marriage relationship. The relationship will die if it doesn't get the time and energy it deserves. It is tragic when a good marriage becomes a business relationship because other priorities have crowded it out.

The key to rebuilding a business marriage into a vibrant marriage is to give focused attention to meeting your spouse's needs (loving him or her). If you learn how to meet your spouse's needs at a new level and with renewed freshness, your spouse will be drawn toward you.

Look at all of your relationships to see if any one of them is choking out time, energy, or resources for your marriage. These are the relationships of your life: God, self, marriage, family, work, church, money, society, friends, and enemies. Make sure the two of you are watching your finances, your parenting strategies, and your work/life balance. Do not remain financially unconscious and just spend whatever comes in. Have a plan and a goal with your money that both of you agree on. Build into your family the essential four R's: respect, responsibility, rules, relationship. It is impossible to have a great marriage if work is always vacuuming up the time and energy. There must be reasonable boundaries that work for both of you.

The Five Problems of Marriage

Ignoring Needs	Immature Behaviors	Clashing Temperaments	Competing Relationships	Past Baggage
Wife's Needs	**Level 1**	**Male vs. Female**	God	
Honor	Thoughtless Immaturity		Self	
Understanding		**Myers-Briggs Temperament**	Marriage	
Security	**Level 2**		Family	
Building Unity	Directed Immaturity	**Ancient Temperament**	Work	
Agreement				
Nurture	**Level 3**	**Love Languages**	Church	
Defender	Destructive, and/or Addictive Immaturity		Money	
Husband's Needs			Society	
Respect	**Eight Solutions**		Friends	
Adaptation	Stop Further Immaturity		Enemies	
Domestic Leadership	Apology			
Intimacy	Alignment			
Companionship	Thoughtful Requests			
Attractive Soul and Body	More Love			
Listener	Change Behavior			
	Clarify			
	Patience			

Problem #5

Past Baggage

Problem #5

Past Baggage

Col. 3:13; Phil. 3:8, 13; Eph. 4:31, 32

Overview

Bill and Carol came to see me because the spark had gone out of their marriage. They were living separate lives, raising their children in a business relationship with absolutely no love in their marriage. At first I approached this as any normal marriage problem in which they were not meeting each other's needs. I gave assignments and required homework so that both would have their needs met on a deeper level, but it wasn't working. They were doing the assignments, but the spark did not return. It was as if every time they lit the flame of their love, a huge bucket of cold water was thrown on the relationship and coldness returned.

I began asking questions about Bill and Carol's past. I thought the difficulty might lie with Bill because he was a very shy and reserved man. But as we probed a little deeper, it was Carol who had suffered a deep wound when her parents divorced. She had never really processed the wound but rather had internally decided her parents' divorce was her fault. If she had been a better daughter, they would have stayed together. She dedicated herself to being the perfect child, but they never reunited. Her parents' divorce had so deeply affected her that she found it impossible to let herself respond to her husband. She secretly believed he would leave her as the children were growing up. When her own children neared the age she was when her parents divorced, she unconsciously hardened herself from the blow she knew was coming. She expected him to announce he was divorcing her and she would have to raise the children alone—just as her mother had done.

Her internal pain was operating as a self-fulfilling prophecy. She erected barriers to love and response, so she was slowly driving her husband away. The fact that she hadn't openly processed her parents' divorce put her on autopilot to recreate the same damage in her own marriage.

Thankfully, when this was pointed out, she was willing to process her parents' divorce, its causes, and its ramifications. Several times she sobbed deeply in my office as she walked through various aspects of the divorce and its aftermath. Those tears were a necessary part of the grieving process. She had never grieved the loss of her family as a child. As an adult, she finally dealt with the past, so it no longer spewed out toxic emotions. It wasn't easy and it took longer than she expected, but it was well worth it. She is now able to give and receive love without fearing divorce as inevitable.

The Fifth Element in Marital Intelligence

The fifth component of Marital Intelligence is unearthing and dealing with past baggage issues. There are at least three types of past baggage issues that consistently come up in marriage counseling:

- Wounds, hurts, abuse, and victimization
- Negative family and cultural programming
- Past actions

We carry with us wounds and destructive internalized programming as well as guilt and consequences from our past actions. There is no way to seal off the past and have its unresolved issues stay away. At times the impact of unresolved past baggage is so strong that it must be dealt with before progress in marriage can be attempted. There may be so much psychological, emotional, and spiritual turmoil created by those issues that it is impossible to be a loving and generous person to one's spouse. It will continue as is unless those wounds are exposed, grieved, and processed.

We must answer the following questions if we are to get a handle on this fifth problem in marriage:

- What traumas, losses, wounds, difficulties, and hurts have I suffered? How might they be affecting my life and marriage?

- What did my family teach me about living that might be damaging my marriage?

- What is my culture directing me to do, say, and think that may be damaging my marriage?

- What have I done in the past that may be impacting my marriage right now?

These questions are very painful to contemplate, but if explored in a safe environment with safe people, the process can be liberating.

When we married, we were convinced we had found the person who could fill up our empty spaces and straighten out our crooked places. We were so excited that finally someone was willing to let us explain our side of the story and see problems from our point of view. While marriage is a wonderful place of healing and hope, it often can't be the complete therapy we need. Our spouse may not be equipped to help or have the patience to wade through all the crud in our lives.

Many people are psychologically, emotionally, or spiritually limping through life. In a number of cases those people end up wounding others because of their issues.

There have been several times I've said to couples in marriage counseling, "I can't fix your marriage until you deal with the issues of your past." I believe that is why there are so many support and recovery groups today. People need to process their pain from the past.

Marital Intelligence Test

This test probes the actions necessary to have a great marriage. Do not be surprised by the results. Celebrate your strengths and start work on improving your weak areas. Your spouse might respond differently to the same questions. The areas of differences are opportunities to grow and improve your marriage. Hopefully this test will whet your appetite for the solutions in this book.

Problem #5

0 = Never; 1 = Rarely; 2 = Occasionally; 3 = Sometimes; 4 = Usually; 5 = Always

I am processing the pain of my past so that it does not damage my marriage.	0 1 2 3 4 5
I am aware and open about the deeply painful things in my life and how they impact my relationships.	0 1 2 3 4 5
I am supportive (financially, emotionally, and relationally) of my spouse's receiving the help he/she needs to overcome the issues and difficulties of his/her past.	0 1 2 3 4 5
I have changed behaviors I learned from my family that were damaging my relationships.	0 1 2 3 4 5
I am open to discussions about unhelpful and/or destructive patterns I have learned from my family.	0 1 2 3 4 5
I am open to discussions about unhelpful and/or destructive patterns I have learned from my culture or heritage.	0 1 2 3 4 5
I have done all I can to bring healing to the destructive behavior in my past so it does not damage my present relationships.	0 1 2 3 4 5
My spouse is aware of and open about the traumatic events of his or her past that impact his or her relationships.	0 1 2 3 4 5
My spouse is processing the pain of his or her past so that it will not damage our marriage.	0 1 2 3 4 5
My spouse is supportive of my receiving the help I need to deal with the issues of my past.	0 1 2 3 4 5
My spouse is open to discussions and change in areas of unhelpful and/or destructive patterns he/she learned from his/her family.	0 1 2 3 4 5

My spouse is open to discussions and change in areas of unhelpful and/or destructive patterns he/she learned from his/her culture or heritage.	0 1 2 3 4 5
My spouse admits foolish, selfish, and/or destructive behaviors of the past and has done all he or she can so that they have the least impact in the present.	0 1 2 3 4 5
Subtotal Section #5	

Add up your total. How did you do? Remember that these results reflect the current condition of your relationship today. Realize, too, that no one is the perfect spouse. You know you haven't been, and you shouldn't expect your husband or wife to be either. You both have weak areas and difficulties in the journey of marriage; but with time and effort, your marriage can improve. The solutions in this book *will* work.

The positive statements you responded to on the test outline a high standard of how we should treat one another. Start applying these truths to your spouse, and your relationship will improve right away.

Scoring

65-52: You have a very good marriage in this area. Keep it up. If there are areas you need to explore, develop a plan to work through them, so you can give and receive love more effectively.

51-39: You have a good marriage that could be improved by facing some of the issues this section brings up. Develop a plan to work through your past baggage issues, so you can give and receive love more effectively. Your spouse may not be the safest person to begin the process with; a trusted friend, counselor, pastor, or psychologist may be a better choice.

38-24: One or both spouses need to put some serious time into addressing issues of the past, or your marriage will not reach its potential. You are most likely limping now and moving into a bad, business-type marital relationship.

23-0: There are significant past baggage issues impacting your marriage. Seek out a counselor, pastor, or psychologist to begin a process of working through these issues so that your marriage does not fail. There is hope and there is help.

Type One – Past Baggage: Wounds and Victimization

There are more, but in marriage counseling three types of past baggage seem to predominate. Bill and Carol's story might be labeled Wounds, Abuse, or Victimization of the Past. This is the first type of past baggage issues. In some cases, it was a molestation that took place when the individual was young. In other cases, it was the death of a parent. Perhaps it was a parental divorce. Perhaps it was guilt and trauma suffered as a teen or young adult. In some cases, it is covered over by an addiction that prevents dealing with the wound. All of these and others can rise to the level of a dominant marriage issue so that nothing can be done to make a significant improvement in the marriage until the issues are addressed.

Many times we bury those painful and devastating episodes. But often it takes only a small thing to trigger the horror of our past. At some point we must deal with the pain, loss, and torment. If we do not deal with those issues, they can sabotage a good marriage. I have watched people who ignore the past, divorce one spouse, and go on the hunt for the next spouse without dealing with the cancer. The answer is never another spouse. Until you deal with the issues of your younger years, you can't have a healthy relationship of loving and being loved.

Healing Abuse, Wounds, and Victimization

Brenda and her husband, Darrell, came to see me because their marriage was falling apart. They had settled into a cold business-like marriage and were hoping the spark could return. Both of them wanted the passionate romance that marked their dating period and the beginning of their marriage. They came to counseling half-expecting me to reveal that this is what marriages are like once you have teenagers. It was once great; now live in the memory of the good old days, and enjoy bland oatmeal relations until you die. As we began working through the counseling process, the normal exercises were having no effect. He felt she was frigid towards him in the bedroom. She admitted she didn't like sex and tried to avoid it as much as possible. As we worked on improving their marriage relationship, it became evident she was not operating from a level playing field. A major issue in their marriage was sexual relations. The normal assignments and exercises in this area were not working. She finally revealed she had been repeatedly molested by her stepfather when she was in her early teens. Eventually, she ran away from home and was abused by a series of boyfriends. The emotional, mental, and spiritual scars from these victimizations were destroying her marriage. If she did not process these traumas, her marriage could not improve. Thankfully, she and her husband were willing to walk slowly through those past wounds to significantly heal her response to sexual intimacy.

It is important to process pain and trauma; otherwise we can become a twisted and distorted version of who we should be. It is not without reason that Jesus said, "Blessed are those who mourn, for they shall be comforted." We must learn how to walk through a process of forgiveness so the trauma of the past does not poison the future.

While people want their spouse to be the one who quietly walks them through whatever fixes they need to make, it won't work in more traumatic situations. A spouse doesn't usually have listening skills or understanding of the steps that bring healing. If you have been through significant trauma in your past, you must process this pain and the choices you made because of it. If the trauma was deep, repetitive, or criminal, then it is important to get professional help to process with you. The earlier in your life these events took place, the more impacting the events can be. I have spent hundreds of hours listening to the horrible things that parents, uncles, friends, babysitters, stepparents, neighbors, and other trusted adults have said and done to young children. Those events cannot be swept under the rug forever. While God may give us the gift of denial when we are young, those traumas need to be dealt with later and drained of their power. I remember women and men crying over why they could no longer ignore the awful pain that happened in their family. But God in His mercy has allowed flashbacks and memories, so the victim would process the trauma as an adult. People need to grieve, seek justice, evaluate, understand, confront, clarify, and forgive others and themselves. There may be a point at which all other activity has to take a back seat to processing those traumas.

One of my favorite questions for getting at issues is, "Have you ever been deeply hurt or wounded by someone you trusted?" It is a powerful question when asked in a setting where I can listen to people's stories. It is not a question to ask flippantly in a crowd or when in a hurry. It is a question to ask when there is time to listen. I have found that when I ask it with kindness and gentleness, people will tell their story. At some point in the listening process I ask, "Would you like to begin processing this pain in your life?" or "Would you be open to learning how to let go of this pain?" The person has to be willing to let go of the thing that has defined him for a large portion of his life. If a person is using his trauma as the defining moment of his life, the devil has him bound and gagged. He must want to be free.

Listen to what Hebrews 12:15 says about the issue of forgiveness. "See to it that no one comes short of the grace of God; that no root of bitterness springing up causes trouble, and by it many be defiled" (NASB).

God gives grace to the wounded. He expects us to use His grace to release the trauma so the wound does not destroy us. We were never designed to carry hatred, bitterness, and anger without doing serious damage to ourselves. Learn how to release it, and let it go.

Learning to forgive is about processing your wound, hurt, loss, and pain. It takes time. It means you must look at your pain from different angles and begin moving it from inside your soul to the outside world. It is a process of bringing your secret pain and damage into the light of the real world. Sometimes actions must be taken against the people who hurt you. Sometimes you will find you've had an inaccurate picture of the loss or wound. Sometimes it will mean taking a fresh look at what took place and gaining a new level of understanding from it.

Processing your pain means getting some emotional distance away from it. That can happen only when the pain comes out of you through writing, talking, or discussing it. The event retains its power over you through hidden mental traps, seductions, faulty perspectives, and dangerous connections as long as you keep it inside. But when you walk through a process to bring your wounds outside of you, they will lose much of their destructive force.

Many times we don't want to take the time or energy to pull apart the ball of emotions, pain, anger, and even truth that sits like a toxic tumor in the center of our souls. We want to pretend it isn't there, but eventually it must be separated and drained of its power. We must separate fact from fiction. We must look at what actually took place and not believe the shadowy monster we have concocted in our minds.

There are only a few basic exercises in this chapter. I would highly recommend, if you have had trauma or victimization in your past, to begin working with a pastor, spiritual director, life coach, counselor, or psychologist.

The Steps to Forgiveness

It is crucial to let go of wounds and hurts of the past in an intelligent and freeing process. It isn't done through denial and filling our lives with something else as we'd like to believe. Failure to forgive has significant physical, mental, emotional, and spiritual consequences. We must choose to walk through a process of forgiveness even though what the other person did was immoral, terrible, and devastating. I heard a definition of bitterness that is priceless. Bitterness is like drinking a bottle of poison and expecting the other person to die. We didn't choose to be wounded. We didn't cause what was done to us, but we are significantly damaged by the impact of those actions. Yet, we still have to walk through a process of forgiveness, or those deeds will have an even greater impact in our lives. We must be set free.

Step 1: Identify the people that have wounded you, what they did, and when it happened.

How do we begin to get a handle on the hurt and pain in our life? We start by giving them a name, a time, and a description. That sounds almost too simplistic, but it is a very good way to begin. Make a list of the people who have deeply hurt or wounded you over the course of your life. You may think the list will be endless, but I have found that usually an individual has been deeply wounded in his life by fewer than two-dozen people. There may be others who have offended him or her, but the big perpetrators number 20 or fewer.

We begin the process of forgiving as emotional explorers—like crime scene investigators looking for the driver of the truck that hit you. We want the name of the driver, a description of the truck he was driving, the date it took place, and eventually what caused him to hit you (motive). Later you will look at how his actions affected you.

Like being hit by a huge truck, when we are deeply wounded we can scarcely believe it. It takes a long time to heal. We may never be the same again. The scars of the accident are still evident in so many ways. Many times it wasn't even an accident.

Actually sitting down and making a list of who, what, and when brings a level of clarity and finiteness to the pain that has permeated your life for so long. At times this process is so painful that you will be flooded with emotions as you recall what took place. That's okay; it's a part of the healing process. Don't try to complete the whole list in one sitting if it becomes too overwhelming. If you need to write more details of the story to get it out, that's helpful. Many times a journalistic account of the events needs to be recorded to make progress. It may take pages of details and research to see if your memory serves you correctly. I have allowed only a small space in this book for those entries, so I recommend using a journal to complete the assignments.

Writing out the details of the trauma will be extremely helpful, but it is maximally helpful when a safe, caring person hears your account as well. It may be a close and trusted friend. It may be a counselor or therapist. It may be a pastor. It must be someone who is safe and loving. If a person is flippant and uninterested when you share, find someone else as your listener and confidant, even if it is your spouse. This is too important to trust someone who doesn't know how to listen. Your confidant should not try to justify the perpetrator's actions. He or she should not expect that you should be over it by now. Your confidant shouldn't butt in about difficult times he or she has endured. His or her purpose should be to explore the pain in your life.

It is important to identify the specific people who have hurt you rather than leaving the wound undefined. When a wound is not hooked to a specific person, it seems to gather other hurts and slights to bolster its case. Usually, this ball of bitterness began as a specific hurt by an individual but over time grew to a huge radioactive area that prevents objectivity toward others.

Every time we can purge our pain outside of ourselves, it helps the process of removing toxins from our lives. When the list is written out, things become much clearer. Also, having a finite number of people who are the source of your pain is often very significant.

Forgiveness Exercise

Who deeply hurt or wounded you?	What did they do?	When?

Now that you've written your list, it is helpful to have someone ask you about these various incidents so you can fill out the story. A counselor or a trusted friend who will listen without judgment can do it. Remember that processing means purging your pain from the inside of your soul to the outside world. Once outside, it can be declawed and defanged, greatly contributing to lesser pain.

Step 2: Determine what type of offense it was *(Luke 23:34; Acts 16:35-40; Matt. 18:15-18; Col. 3:13; Acts 6:1-3).*

There are all types of offenses. Some are criminal, requiring the authorities to step in so that type of offense does not recur. Some offenses are civil in which fines and minor punishments are imposed by a local agency. Some offenses are unethical or immoral and, therefore, need to be reprimanded by the church or community. Some offenses are family offenses, requiring a family to deal with the wrongdoing and correct the behavior. Some offenses are personal, requiring interaction about the problem. Some offenses are normal, everyday slights and selfishness that require love to overlook.

Types of offenses:

- Criminal
- Civil
- Organizational
- Accidental
- Familial
- Personal
- Everyday

It is important that we classify correctly the offenses that have thrust themselves into our lives. Some require the use of outside agents for justice and objectivity. Some require clarification of expectations rather than involving other people in our hurt. I have seen people turn personal offenses into life-changing hatred because they won't communicate properly. I have also heard people describe horrible crimes committed against them, yet they have allowed the perpetrator to continue hurting others.

Forgiveness Exercise

Work through the process of actually classifying the offenses that have wounded you and kept you from emotional and spiritual freedom.

Who offended, wounded, or hurt you?	Which kind of offense? Criminal, civil, organizational, accidental, familial, personal, everyday	What action needs to be taken to stop, process, or fix this offense?

It is not enough to classify these offenses, although in many cases it brings great insight and relief. It is important that you take appropriate actions in response to the offense. Seek counsel and prayer, but do not be afraid to take appropriate action to stop this kind of offense from happening again.

Step 3: Confess your sins *(1 John 1:9).*

Often a wound is connected in some way to an offense on our part. We may not like to admit this, but we may have had some culpability. We triggered or helped produce an offense against us. We may have excused our part as minor, but something we did or said is involved.

> Dear Heavenly Father,
>
> I come to You in the name of the Lord Jesus Christ. I realize I should not have done _____. I realize it was wrong and agree with what you say in the Bible about that type of action. I ask that you apply the work of Christ on the cross to my actions in this area. Thank you for forgiving my sin in Christ. I don't want to do this anymore. Please energize me to go in a different direction when I am offered this kind of choice again. Make me into the person you want me to be. As much as possible I want to repair the damage I've done.
>
> Thank you for your offer of forgiveness in Christ. I admit I need it, and I accept your transforming power to act differently in the future.
>
> In the name of the Lord Jesus Christ, Amen.

Forgiveness Exercise

Look at your previous lists and assign any responsibility to yourself. It may be as small as one percent. Mark it down. There may also be separate offenses you caused that need to be cleansed before you can continue in the healing process.

Who?	What did they do?	Classification	When?	Percent of Your Fault/ Blame

It has been tough sledding and difficult work up to this point, but it is crucial that these offenses be brought into the light of day and examined. The above process may take weeks and involve deep, emotional pain. Bitterness is like a cockroach that does its dirty work in the dark. When exposed to the light, it shrivels up, and its hold on your life is greatly diminished. If you've worked through the past few assignments, bitterness is already losing its grip.

Hidden wounds are the source of addictions. Addictions are a form of running from painful memories or events. Addictions self-medicate so that we don't have to face the wound. Layer upon layer of alcohol, drugs, sex, or food is placed upon the wound, so it recedes into the background of our lives. But all the while, unexamined wounds are poisoning our souls. They demand that we seek more forms of self-medication to avoid thinking about them. They force us down a path laden with destructive choices and damaged relationships. Unexamined wounds force us to become as self-focused as the offenders were when they wounded us. Do not let bitterness win! Bring the offense out into the open. Examine what happened. Take action against the wound. Allow the healing water of God's grace and mercy to cleanse your wound.

Forgiveness Exercise

I recommend you memorize a little six-sentence apology to use when you are seeking to clear up your offenses. Using this type of apology may take a while as the person may need to detail how you hurt him or her and the consequences of your actions. Listening with patience and nondefensiveness is the best way to bring about a restored relationship. Adapt this apology to clear up those who have been offended by you.

> Recently God has caused me to realize how much I hurt you when _____ happened. I'm sure I don't know all the ways I hurt you by doing what I did. But I don't want to hurt anyone else this way, so I hope you'll help me understand how I hurt you. (A long time of listening may be required to understand the offended person's point of view.) Thank you for helping me understand more clearly what I did. I realize I was wrong. I know I don't have any right to ask, but will you forgive me?

Step 4: By an act of your will specifically forgive those who have deeply wounded and hurt you (Matthew 18:33).

Jesus spends considerable time talking with His disciples about for-giveness. He advises that we should have an attitude of forgiveness toward the selfishness of others because the Lord has forgiven us.

Matthew 18:33 says, "Should you not also have had mercy on your fellow slave, in the same way that I had mercy on you?" We have been given an entrance ticket into heaven that is of the highest value. We could never earn it or deserve it. It has been given to us because of the graciousness of God. He paid the price for our forgiveness. He sought us out and drew us to Him when He could have left us to wander in our lost estate. If we've been given this treasure, we should be able to forgive our fellow man.

In a sense, it's like we've won the eternal lottery. We have been granted, through no work on our part, the gift of eternal life. We have been chosen, forgiven, and awarded the ultimate prize where God will make all things new. How can we not forgive others when we have been granted this incredible gift?

Forgiveness Exercise

When thoughts of bitterness or vengeance return to your mind, repeat the phrase, "I have chosen to forgive _____ and leave with God any education, punishment, or vengeance of _____," or "My current responsibility is to love the people God has placed in my life." It is very helpful to reinforce a commitment to forgiveness to the Lord through prayer.

Dear Heavenly Father,

I choose to forgive _____ for what He (or she) did to me. God, You have forgiven me in Christ and have washed me clean of my many offenses against You. How can I not forgive _____ for what he (or she) did to me?

In the name of the Lord Jesus Christ, Amen.

Step 5: Make a list of good things that have come or could come from this offense (Romans 8:28).

The Bible says God is all-powerful. He can redirect the flow of an offense into a blessing if we love Him and move in the direction of His will for us. What others have done doesn't need to destroy us, but it can be used by God to open up whole new avenues of opportunity. Start looking for them.

A young woman came to see me because she was deeply wounded by a former boyfriend. I asked her to make a list of all the good and bad things that came from what he did. She had an easy time listing the bad, but she couldn't think of many good things God could do because of those offenses. It took much coaching and weeks of list-making before she could make a list twice as long of the good things. When the list of the positives became twice as long as the negatives, she began to see the offense in a whole new light. For the first time, she could pray about cooperating with all the good God could do.

Initially, she wanted me to condemn the young man and/or figure a way for her to get back together with him. She was convinced she would never marry after this because she couldn't trust men. A number of years later, however, she did marry a wonderful man and is enjoying a beautiful family.

Forgiveness Exercise

What are the bad things that have come from this offense?

1.	6.
2.	7.
3.	8
4.	9.
5.	10.

What are the positives that God has brought or could bring out of this offense?

1.	11.
2.	12.
3.	13
4.	14.
5.	15.
6.	16.
7.	17.
8.	18.
9.	19.
10.	20.

An even list will not release you, for the negatives are more powerful. You need a list at least twice as long of the good to mentally embrace this new reality. God is about doing something incredible with you—even through your messes.

Step 6: Educate the offender about the offense (Luke 17:3, Matt. 18:15-18).

Look at what Jesus teaches in Luke 17:3-4: "Be on your guard! If your brother sins, rebuke him; and if he repents, forgive him. And if he sins against you seven times a day, and returns to you seven times, saying, 'I repent,' forgive him." Jesus is teaching that an important part of forgiveness is to address both sides of the offense. Interestingly enough, the disciples' reaction to Jesus' command was to exclaim, "Increase our faith!"

The Bible speaks regularly about rebuking those who offend you. We don't understand this idea, but it is powerful. When done in a spirit of gentleness and humility, it can produce a dramatic effect.

A rebuke is a strong form of education. One way to describe rebuking is to see it as an alignment of expectations. When someone offends you, he or she has behaved in an unexpected way. It is important to let the offener know you need to align expectations with him or her. When he or she did _____ or _____, it was not appropriate. A rebuke is helping the other person understand how it felt to be on the other end of what the offender said or did. It helps the offender realize there are consequences to his or her actions. It does not allow the person to remain blissfully ignorant about the offending behavior.

A rebuke must be done in the right way, at the right time, and in a safe environment. I have seen a dramatic effect on the wounded when they stand up to educate their offender. Do not do this if you would put yourself in further physical, emotional, spiritual, or mental danger, and make sure you know what you will say. Just spewing emotion at your offender doesn't help. There must be truth, consequences, and impact in a rebuke.

Whom should you educate about their offense?	What will you say?

These are simple little boxes on a piece of paper; but when you take the time to fill them out, they can help to free you from the grip of bitterness.

Type Two - Past Baggage:
Negative Family and Cultural Programming

The second aspect of past baggage is family and cultural programming we use to direct our lives. Most of us don't realize that we act, react, and live our lives in ways similar to our extended families. Some of these unevaluated ways are destructive to our relationships, but we never connect the consequences (constant anger, inability to discuss issues, sexual difficulties, physical violence, belittling) with a family behavior because it feels natural. It is the way we've always acted. I'm amazed how many people yell at their spouse when asked a question mainly because they don't know to act any other way. I have watched men and women turn and walk away from their spouse rather than deal with a difficult subject or lose an argument. That is the way they saw their family deal with those things, so they naturally do the same. I have watched in horror as husbands and wives have affairs when they are lonely in their marriages because that is what they saw their parents do. I have watched couples vehemently argue over money, repeating the same arguments their parents had rather than looking for a solution. I have watched people play the martyr card when they don't get their way—just like their parents did. If we're not careful, we will follow the last programming we experienced whether it was effective or not.

Looking at this aspect of past baggage means looking at the family and cultural commands about key areas of life. We need to examine default responses to see if they're the most effective. Cultures and families gave us the default programs that will continue running despite the fact that they don't work. In fact, they tend to inflame situations or destroy relationships. It is easy to overlook the impact of these hidden ways of acting and speaking. We must examine and evaluate whether they are effective. Learning a new way of acting, responding, and speaking in various situations is difficult but well worth it.

Family and Cultural Programming

Beth took on a martyr attitude every time she felt her husband or children weren't pitching in to help as she thought they should. This infuriated her husband and often caused him to walk away. "Why do you do that? Just ask us to help," he told her. It took some time to figure out she was mimicking the way her mother tried to get her father to help. Beth didn't remember this attitude as especially effective for her mother, but it was the way she had seen it handled. It took Beth's conscious effort to end the manipulation and simply ask. It didn't feel natural at first, but it did cause her husband to be more helpful.

John and Sharon were on the verge of separation and potential divorce. They came to counseling convinced their problems were insurmountable. As I began to probe and learn about their marriage, it became evident that much of the disagreement came from Saturday mornings. Sharon came from a family of early risers. Her parents were up Saturday morning at the crack of dawn to do chores. The attitude was if you didn't do that, you were lazy and wouldn't amount to much. John, on the other hand, came from a family of late risers on Saturday and Sunday. His family lounged around in their pajamas on their only days to sleep in. They had leisurely breakfasts late into the morning and watched cartoons. Any chores were put off until after lunch. They wanted to enjoy the morning.

Both John and Sharon were operating out of their family programming; they just didn't realize it. Saturday morning and a hundred other little preferences were clashing and ruining their marriage. When they realized they were not right or wrong issues but merely preferences, their marriage got on the right track. Sometimes one person needed to bend. Sometimes the other needed to bend. Sometimes a new idea needed to be pursued.

All of us have received many good and bad things from our families. We received from our families an unexamined gift, a software program on how to do life. Even if we don't agree with our parents, we received their operating system and without realizing it we often carry out life the same way they did.

I am deeply grateful for the in-depth work that Pete Scazzero has done in this area. His books *Emotionally Healthy Spirituality*[1] and *The Emotionally Healthy Church,*[2] have been groundbreaking in examining hidden past baggage that disrupts the present. I highly recommend reading and working through these books. He deals with this material much more thoroughly than I can in this small section. Through these books, I have realized that all of us have unexamined past baggage.

It is extremely helpful for couples to have discussions about the messages and guidance their families furnished in crucial areas. It is enlightening for individuals to look at how they are engineered when dealing with certain topics and activities. All of a sudden there is an "aha" moment when the person says, "I'm doing the same things my dad did," or "I'm just doing what I saw my parents do!" At this point, people can realize what their parents employed may not have worked then and won't work now.

It is after the "aha" moment that a person can consciously begin to change. We don't have to replay our parents' solutions. We don't have to follow the default settings we were programmed with to handle our marriage. It takes work to choose to act, speak, react, and think differently; but it can be done. We can choose to be different. We can look at various ways to behave and implement a new behavior that actually produces the results we desire.

I have had the privilege of introducing new strategies and behaviors to hundreds of married couples. Applying these ideas always produces a new level of love and joy in a marriage. We must realize that if what we're currently doing is not working, *we* must change instead of hoping our spouse will change. It is possible to have a successful marriage, full of joy; but it takes willingness to adjust what we do, what we say, and how we think. We have control over each of those things.

Early Childhood Programming:
What Did Your Family Unconsciously Teach You About _____?

We are going to use Scazzero's categories but add specific questions to help you explore these areas. Your family may have given you a wonderful system of handling issues or a completely dysfunctional system. You, however, need to examine the system so you can determine if it needs to be refined, replaced, or reinforced. This process can be enlightening and sometimes life changing.

The initial work can be done alone or with your spouse. At times the information can become so emotionally charged that it may need to be processed with a counselor, but bringing light to the hidden operating system directing your behavior is key to developing a successful marriage.

Marriage Solutions and Exercises

Use the questions below to gain a clear picture of what your parents taught you in these crucial areas. The questions are designed to be discussion starters, not comprehensive evaluation questions for each category. You may go way beyond those questions or not even need them. As you talk your way through those questions with your spouse or a counselor, write down key phrases, actions, or messages under each heading. This will crystallize your insight into the systems your parents passed on to you.

1. *Money*

How did your parents handle money?

What were your parents' mottos and attitudes toward money?

What did your parents teach or model about making money?

What did your parents teach or model about managing money?

What did your parents teach or model about giving money?

In what ways are you handling money the same way your parents did?

What do you believe is the best way of making money?

What do you believe is the best way of managing money?

What do you believe is the best way of giving money?

2. *Success*

What did your parents teach or model about being successful in life?

What messages did your parents give you about success in life?

How did your parents try to become successful?

What was your parents' success plan?

What do you believe is the best definition of success?

3. *Feelings*

How did your family deal with feelings and/or expressed emotions (i.e., crying, shouting, screaming, anger, hatred)?

What did your parents say about people who expressed feelings or emotions?

How do you handle feelings? Is it as your parents did?

What do you believe is the best way of expressing your emotions?

4. *Roles of Men and Women*

How did your parents model the roles for men and women?

How would you like your mate to act?

How close does your ideal mate conform to the actions of your parents?

What did your parents teach or model about how a man should behave?

What did your parents teach or model about how a woman should behave?

What do you believe is God's role for men and women?

5. *Physical Affection*

How physically affectionate were your parents?

Did they say anything about public displays of affection?

What do you believe is the best way of displaying affection?

6. *Compliments and Praise*

When did you receive compliments or praise from your parents?

What did your parents teach or model to you about compliments or praise?

What was the greatest compliment or praise you ever received from your parents?

What do you believe is the best way to handle compliments and praise?

7. *Sexual Relations*

How did your parents deal with sexual relations?

What did they say or do to teach you about sexual relations?

What do you believe is the best way to handle sexual expression in marriage?

8. *Loss and Grief*

How did your family handle grief and significant loss?

What did your parents teach or model about times of significant loss?

How long did your parents allow themselves to process significant loss?

What do you believe is the best way to handle significant loss?

9. *Expressing Anger*

How did your parents express anger?

What did your parents do when someone expressed anger?

What did your parents teach or model about expressing anger?

What do you believe is the best way to express anger?

10. *Parenting and Children*

What did your parents do to train or control their children?

What did your parents say about their role as parents or your role as children?

What was communicated about having children (joy, duty, drudgery)?

What do you believe is the best way of parenting children?

11. *God and Religion*

What did your parents model about God and religion?

What did your parents teach or say about God and religion?

What do you believe is the best way of dealing with God and religion?

12. *Conflict*

How did your family deal with conflict?

How was conflict resolved?

What did your family do if someone remained in conflict?

What do you believe is the best way of handling family conflict?

13. *Marriage and Singleness*

What did your family say or teach about being married or single?

How did your family treat married couples and single people?

Was singleness an acceptable goal?

Was marriage the ultimate goal?

What do you believe is the better marital status?

14. *Pleasure, Recreation, and Fun*

What did your family do for fun?

What activities did your family allow for fun?

How much money and time was given to pleasure, recreation, or fun?

What do you believe is the best balance of work and recreation?

15. *Race, Culture, and Class*

What did your family communicate to you about your race, culture, or class?

What did your family communicate to you about others of a different race, culture, or class?

What do you believe is the best way to interact with race, culture, or class?

16. *Authorities and Power*

What did your parents model in relation to authorities?

What did your parents teach or say about authorities?

How did your parents react to an authority stopping them from doing something?

17. *Politics*

What was your parents' attitude toward politics?

What did your parents say about politics?

What were your parents' political views?

What do you believe is the best approach to politics?

The key question in this arena is, "Are you following your parents' way of relating and interacting in a given area, or are you following God's way of relating and interacting?" We all are following some programming that either helps us or hurts us.

Cultural Influences and Commandments

If we are going to enjoy a great marriage, we must understand how our culture tries to install an operating system for how to do life. Unfortunately, our culture's idea for how to handle certain aspects of life is no better than our family's idea. The goal for a good marriage is knowing how to take delight in each other, not knowing how to win. Too often our culture feeds the idea, "Win at the other person's expense." In marriage, if one loses because the other wins, both lose. We need to fight our way through our past and present cultural programming to choose the most effective strategy for our relationships.

We must realize there are messages every culture sends that sabotage a good marriage. Some cultures tell men that unfaithfulness is normal, expected, and even necessary to have a healthy life. Some cultures tell women not to express themselves. Some cultures tell men never to let their wives speak. Some cultures tell women they need to be the boss of the family because men are stupid. Some cultures direct men and women to avoid communication, honesty, and faithfulness, and the list goes on. Some cultures expect men to cheat sexually on their wives. Some cultures tell wives not to adapt to their husbands. Some cultures tell men it is okay to beat their wives when they are angry or displeased. Christians must guard against unhealthy cultural influences.

A number of men I have counseled pushed back when I told them how to improve their marriage. "I can't do that! If I were to do that, I would be a hen-pecked husband." "My brothers would never let me live it down if I listened to what my wife said in their presence." Even though I show them in Scripture that God instructs men to honor their wives above their parents and extended families, it takes significant time to act on programming different from what they received from their cultural background.

The question is, do you have ways of treating your spouse that are undermining the great marriage you want? If we lined up your actions toward your spouse with what the Bible says a husband or a wife should do, would your actions agree with the Bible or your culture? Too often our actions line up with our specific cultural norms for marital behavior instead of Christ's new programming for us. It feels right to do what everyone else is doing; but when we follow the norms, we end up with the same marriage problems.

Think about the problems you have in your marriage: money, in-laws, sexual issues, breakdown of communication, or stubbornness, to name a few. Many times the reason you have those problems is because you are dealing with them the way your culture has trained you. Could it be that you are unconsciously following cultural programming that won't work in the real world? If you do that, there often is no solution to the problems in your marriage.

What are destructive cultural messages?

Slogans, mottos, and cultural proverbs are reflections of a cultural mindset and can become a default operating system. The following are some modern slogans that reflect a cultural mindset:

"You only go around once in life."
"Look out for #1."
"You deserve it."
"Don't deprive yourself."
"The one with the most toys at the end wins."
"Obey your thirst."
"Party On!"
"Did you get the latest?"
"Everyone wants to be rich and famous."
"I don't submit to anyone."
"It's my money."
"This makes me happy."
"I did it my way."
"Yeah, I told them!"

If you watch enough television, you can pick up a completely skewed picture of how to have a good marriage. Everyone is sarcastic, back-stabbing each other, and they play a laugh track for every joke. People are tempted to be unfaithful, and there are few or no consequences if they give in. It is normal for couples to divorce; everyone goes through three or four spouses before they get it right. Children are adaptable. They are not affected by divorce. Men are stupid and should be treated as such. Instead of discussing a topic in private, people wait until a social setting to air dirty laundry, so the other person can't fight back. Marriage is a temporary, man-made institution; get into it only if you feel like it.

What does our culture tell us to do?

Use this exercise to examine what your culture is telling you and how it wants to conform you to its way of thinking. Is this the best way?

1. Money
   What does your culture say is the right way to make money?

What does your culture say is the right way to manage money?
What does your culture say is the right way to give money?

2. *Success*

What is your culture's definition of success?
What does your culture tell you about how to become successful?

3. *Feelings*

What does your culture tell you about expressing your feelings?
How do you express your feelings?

4. *Roles of Men and Women*

What does your culture say is a man's role?
What does your culture say is a woman's role?
What do you believe are the roles of men and women in marriage?

5. *Physical Affection*

What does your culture say is proper physical affection?
How do you display physical affection to your spouse?

6. *Compliments and Praise*

What does your culture say is the right way to compliment your spouse?
How do you praise and compliment your spouse?

7. *Sexual Relations*

What does culture say is the right amount of sexual relations in marriage?
What does your partner think is the right amount of sexual relations?
What do you believe is the right amount of sexual relations in marriage?

8. *Loss and Grief*

What does your culture say is the right way to express grief and loss?
What do you believe is the best way to process loss and grief?

9. *Expressing Anger*

What does your culture say is the right way to deal with anger?
What do you believe is the best way to deal with anger?

10. *Parenting and Children*
   What does your culture say is the right way to parent children?
   What do you believe is the best way to parent children?

11. *God and Religion*
   What does your culture say is right in this area?
   What do you believe is the best way to deal with God and religion?

12. *Conflict*
   What does your culture say is the right way to deal with conflict in marriage?
   What do you believe is the best way to deal with conflict in marriage?

13. *Marriage and Singleness*
   What does your culture tell you about marriage and singleness?
   What do you believe is the appropriate orientation to marriage and singleness?

14. *Pleasure, Recreation, and Fun*
   What does your culture tell you about pleasure and recreation?
   What do you believe is the best way to handle this area?

15. *Race, Culture, and Class*
   What does your culture tell you about race, culture, and class?
   What do you believe is the best way to handle race, culture, and class?

16. *Authorities and Power*
   What does your culture tell you about authority and power?
   What do you believe is the best approach to authority and power?

17. *Politics*
   What does your culture tell you about politics?
   What do you believe is the best approach to politics?

Type Three – Past Baggage: Past Actions

The third aspect of baggage issues is past courses and choices you've made. Many people have done things they feel deeply guilty about.

The guilt impacts every part of their lives, whether they know it or not. I know of men who forced previous girlfriends to have abortions years ago, and it still drips toxic acid into their lives. I have watched past infidelities twist the ability to enjoy a spouse. I know of men and women who have committed heinous acts, and the poisonous guilt spills into every area of their lives, destroying relationships along the way. They need to process their actions by learning to evaluate situations, confessing the wrong done, and finding forgiveness for themselves. If they don't, the memory will continue to haunt them for the rest of their lives.

In movies we see the lie that it's possible for a mafia hit man to kill people in one part of his life but to be a loving and doting family man in another. That does not happen. Life is far more integrated than that. You are the integration point for all parts of your life. If you are guilty of horrible things in one area, they will spill over into other areas.

When we marry, we secretly hope to find a person who will truly accept us for who we are, warts and all. We desire someone who will help us get over stuff from the past that still affects us. Some of us also deeply fear that if our spouse really knew everything, he or she would reject us completely. That can cause large sections of our lives to be off limits to discussion.

We didn't realize that we had brought this unresolved baggage into our marriages, yet it impacts what we say, how we act, and the choices we make. It usually doesn't take long before our mates don't want to listen to another story about our problems; they just want us to behave differently.

Before you were married it was okay for you to have problems in other areas because your lives were not completely intertwined yet, but now your life is your spouse's life, and what you do radically affects him or her. Your spouse may not be able to truly listen and take your perspective like before.

When Jim was a teenager he got his girlfriend pregnant. Rather than deal with the issue head-on, he encouraged her to get an abortion. He helped pay for it and even drove her to the appointment. After her abortion, the relationship fell apart as they both felt guilty. For years Jim tried to hide what he had done. He tried to run away from God and himself. As the years passed, Jim married another young lady, Joanne. He was continually haunted about his relationship with the former girlfriend, the abortion, and his actions in it.

It was not until he acknowledged it was wrong and spoke with his wife about his past that he began to be free from it. Jim realized he needed to face what took place. He accepted responsibility for his actions and pleaded with God to forgive him. God did, and it changed Jim's life. Jim and Joanne began to work together to counsel young women on how to deal with unexpected and unwanted pregnancies. His past became a source of strength for his marriage rather than a constant internal drain. Jim developed a great marriage because he acknowledged his mistakes and made sure they had no impact on his present relationships.

Like Jim, you may hide negative actions over which you feel terribly guilty. Your secrets and guilt may be affecting your marriage. You must process your pain, your guilt, your shame, and your losses. It may not be safe to process these things with your spouse as he or she may not remain objective as your feelings and thoughts spill out. An experienced pastor or counselor can confidentially allow you to work through those issues. If you don't get those past baggage issues out in the open, you are allowing old poison to steal health from your present relationships.

We have all made mistakes. We've committed foolish acts, even harmful, sinful acts. It's important that we don't run from those things but instead acknowledge that we did them, process the pain and guilt, accept God's forgiveness, learn to forgive ourselves, and move on. This reality is a part of our story. It is a process that requires bringing the whole thing into the light of day with a safe person.

I have seen people try to run from their own mistakes. It never works because we carry the memories of what we've done. Some try to hide through alcohol, drugs, pornography, and food. Some even try to hide in activity or religion or compensation, but the real answer is to face what took place and drain the swamp of its alligators. The allure of alcohol, drugs, illicit sex, and other addictions is that they provide only temporary relief from burdens of the past, and the addiction becomes its own burden, twisting and distorting your present and future. Learn to acknowledge the mistakes of your past. There is relief in reality. You don't have to run from this the rest of your life.

Many marriages are troubled by addiction and obsessive behavior. In most cases those destructive behaviors result from some form of hiding from past actions and/or victimizations. The addictive behaviors cause trouble because we have been unwilling to face what really happened. Don't let your marriage be destroyed because you can't face what took place so long ago. Find a safe person and begin talking about it. If you can't find a safe person right away, start writing about your feelings in a journal.

There is incredible power in confession, repentance, openness, and forgiveness. You may be divorced and are forced to send a large portion of your paycheck to your ex. You may have hooked up with a gang and were involved in crime. You may have fathered children you know nothing about. You may have had multiple abortions. You may have pledged yourself to a false god or religion. You may have participated in orgies. You may have been to prison and now live with limiting consequences. You may have been involved in cheating or stealing from your employer, family, or friends. You may have done something that got you banned or barred from your career field. You may be an alcoholic, drug or sex addict, and that has huge implications as you numb out any marital pain through the addiction. You may carry diseases and consequences such as infertility, HIV, pneumonia, allergies, or even multiple personality disorder. All of these problems and many others have been conquered through the power of hope and forgiveness in Christ. There is hope. Whatever was done in the past does not have to derail the present or the future.

Marriage Solutions and Exercises

It is important to acknowledge what you've done. Process the event, pain, and guilt, and accept God's forgiveness; learn to forgive yourself and move on with this reality as part of your story. The following are a few exercises that will help you do it.

Acknowledge Actions of the Past.

What actions and/or conversations have you engaged in that you are ashamed of? Write down a brief description of the incidents. You can't drain those incidents of their power until you get some clear objectivity and then face them. If nothing comes to mind, move on.

Bringing past actions into the light requires a safe person who will hear what happened without being immediately affected by the content. Eventually, you may need to tell others who have a need to know this information, but it is helpful to start with a safe, objective person.

Past actions that need to be exposed	To whom should I reveal these things?

Spend time confessing your wrongdoing to God. Ask for God's forgiveness to be applied to your actions and words. Thank God for His forgiveness. If any restitution is required, begin the process. If there are any civil or criminal penalties required, look into those processes. Your prayer of confession might sound like this:

Dear Heavenly Father,

I come to you as a sinner in need of Your forgiveness. As You know, I _____ (spell out what you did that was wrong). I ask that You apply the blood of Christ and the forgiveness it brings to my actions in this situation. I know I have no right to demand this, but You said if I ask for forgiveness, You give it. Please wash me clean of my sins and allow me to live a life honoring to You.

In the name of the Lord Jesus Christ, Amen.

I have watched people who are willing to face the truth of their past begin to heal as soon as they confess and repent. The process must be worked through in a safe environment with safe people and may take considerable time. It is not a 15-minute quick tune-up but it involves thinking, talking, writing, praying, repenting, crying, and seeking the Lord. To face the fact that you are a sinner, deserving God's punishment, is a huge issue. Realizing that He offers you His forgiveness instead is life-changing. We don't have to live hidden lives of defeat, but we can walk in God's glorious forgiveness.

As you walk in God's forgiveness, you'll be able to incorporate who you are and what you did into the whole of your person, instead of pretending it didn't happen. This is part of the process of forgiving yourself and moving beyond the past. Some of the most saintly people you will ever meet are not perfect people; they are people who admit what they did and now walk in a new reality of God's forgiveness and acceptance.

Facing the Consequences

There are times when what was done needs to be taken beyond just confessing it to God and a safe person. Internal freedom requires justice and truth. At times a spouse may need to know. At times an employer may need to know. At times the proper authorities may need to know. Yes, this kind of admission can destroy marriages, end careers, and even result in jail time, but freedom of the soul is a more valuable commodity. People who continue to hide their past are usually driven by the need to deaden their souls to escape the pain of their past. To be free, they must process and take the appropriate actions about their past.

Determine with a professional whether it is appropriate to tell others about your past actions. Not everyone needs to know it all, but some people may need to know the crucial details about your actions. You will be surprised at what happens when you are free from the burden of hiding and medicating your pain.

Warning: Don't Play the Blame Game

There is often an attempt to put all of the marriage difficulties on the spouse with the most significant past baggage issues. "If he didn't have this issue, our marriage would be great," she says. While it is true that some people have issues that block marital progress, usually that particular issue is not the only reason for a troubled marriage. Most marriages fall apart because the level of love has dropped significantly. It is a high level of love that allows the wounded spouse to tackle past baggage issues. Your spouse fell in love with you because you overlooked his or her idiosyncrasies and loved him or her anyway. Your spouse needs that level of support and help if he or she is going to tackle these huge issues.

Walking through our past is a fearful step. We must take the time to understand the ways our spouse has been damaged by past relationships, actions, and words. When we help our spouse assign the proper amount of blame, justice, and forgiveness, the healing will begin. There is a way of releasing the toxins. We must learn how to drain this poison out of our marriages. Working through the process of forgiveness is extremely powerful.

It seemed Loren and Adriana had a great marriage. Little did they know that lurking beneath the surface was a problem that would shake their marriage to its foundation. Loren was seeking to become a better husband, father, and Christian, so he signed up for a class at church. Topics of discussion were lust, pornography, and impure thoughts. As Loren worked through the material, Adriana asked him if he had ever looked at pornography. He admitted he had some contact with it years before, but it was not a problem at the present time. He was shocked at Adriana's reaction. She came unglued. She yelled. She cried. She demanded he go to sexual addiction counseling. She demanded he sleep in the living room. She didn't want him to touch her. She became emotionally and physically hostile to Loren.

Loren assumed it was his problem and sought help to deal with this problem. What he didn't realize was that Adriana's reaction was more about her than about him. A friend of the family sexually abused Adriana when she was a young girl. This man was heavily into pornography. He had made her look at lots of images during his attacks on her. The whole arena of pornography became supercharged in Adriana's life as pornography meant molestation of young girls. Loren was right to deal with any issues he had regarding the destructive temptations of pornography, but Adriana's reaction suggested there was deep pain she hadn't yet dealt with adequately. As Loren squarely faced his issues, he was able to help Adriana work through the huge issues in her life that were distorting her view of him.

Summary of the Problem of Past Baggage

It is never easy to face unresolved issues, wounds, and emotional programming from our parents or culture, but it is essential. People have varying amounts of past baggage issues. In a culture that has forgotten to set boundaries in life within God's Ten Commandments, we see more and more baggage carried into marriage.

There are three basic forms of past baggage that can destroy a marriage:

- Victimization
- Family and Cultural Programming
- Past Actions.

Look at your life to see what issues you need to face in this area. Don't look at your spouse and his or her issues until you have squarely and honestly looked at these three issues yourself. Take the log out of your own eye before you take the splinter out of your brother's eye (Matt. 7:5).

There is a time when you can help your spouse examine his or her issues. It requires humility, hope, and patience. If the past baggage issues are deep and involved, you will most likely not be the only one who is needed to help your spouse through the issues. Be gracious as well as helpful. Do not enable your spouse's dysfunctional approach to life but rather understand the internal pressures he or she is under. Be a rock of support and hope.

The great danger of a book like this is that the problems can be described quickly and easily and make it seem that the issues can be as quickly resolved. You must realize it may take years to process the hurt, pain, or guilt so that you are free from their destructive power. You have to do the work. You have to find the safe person who will meet with you regularly. You will have to cry, confess, emote, think, and pray your way through the events of your past, so God can pour His forgiveness, hope, and love into your life story. It will be a lot of work, but it's worth it.

If you are the spouse of a person with significant past baggage issues, don't expect that your marriage will immediately improve when your spouse faces these issues. In some cases, the marriage is more difficult as your spouse faces the pain of his or her past. Your understanding and patient love will allow him or her to work through the issue and will ultimately result in a great marriage. Hang in there.

The Five Problems of Marriage

Ignoring Needs	Immature Behaviors	Clashing Temperaments	Competing Relationships	Past Baggage
Wife's Needs	**Level 1**	**Male vs. Female**	**God**	**Type 1** Victimization
Honor	Thoughtless Immaturity		**Self**	
Understanding		**Myers-Briggs Temperament**	**Marriage**	**Type 2** Family and Cultural Programming
Security	**Level 2**			
Building Unity	Directed Immaturity	**Ancient Temperament**	**Family**	
Agreement			**Work**	**Type 3** Past Actions
Nurture	**Level 3**	**Love Languages**	**Church**	
Defender	Destructive, and/or Addictive Immaturity		**Money**	
Husband's Needs			**Society**	
Respect	**Eight Solutions**		**Friends**	
Adaptation	Stop Further Immaturity		**Enemies**	
Domestic Leadership	Apology			
Intimacy	Alignment			
Companionship	Thoughtful Requests			
Attractive Soul and Body	More Love			
Listener	Change Behavior			
	Clarify			
	Patience			

Conclusion

Conclusion

John and Mary couldn't get along. There were things happening between them they didn't understand. They talked past each other instead of to each other. But they hung in there during times of separation and kept learning and kept trying, and eventually, it clicked. First, it was John who began to act in the right way towards Mary. A year later, Mary began to treat John accordingly. They now have what many would call a model marriage. It took work and perseverance. It took a willingness to admit they didn't know how to make it work. John and Mary were so thankful they didn't give up just because it was mired in difficulties. They tried new things and learned much. Now they have a high level of Marital Intelligence that allows them even to help others with their marriages.

Marriage is a wonderful institution designed by God to benefit the individuals, their children, and society. Two people must overcome their natural selfish orientation and commit to making this arrangement work. When it works, it is a wonder to behold. When it doesn't work, it can be hell on earth. Almost everyone feels the urge to connect deeply with someone and share his or her life with that one person. That is how God wired us. I have been working with, working on, and evaluating marriages for more than 30 years. I have come to realize that when certain principles are kept in mind, the wonder of marriage emerges. However, when we become self-focused, critical, overcommitted, unwilling to give, intolerant, bitter, or unwilling to grow, we doom marriage to be something far less than what it is intended to be. Every marriage has great potential for beauty and joy. We entered into marriage with the hope and desire to enjoy deep love and connectedness with our spouse. It's up to us to make it happen.

Remember there are only five problems in marriage. It is important to be intelligent about marriage. Marriage isn't complicated; it just requires constant attention to certain relational principles. It requires that we get along when we don't feel like it. It requires that we go outside ourselves to meet each other's needs. Remember the five problems:

- **Needs/Lack of Love** – Meet the deep relational needs of your spouse.

- **Selfish, Angry, Destructive Immature Behaviors** – Apologize when you are wrong, clarify when there are concerns, constantly align expectations, and love your spouse.

- **Temperament Differences** – Accept your spouse for who he or she is, and your partner may exceed your expectations.

- **Competing Relationships** – Learn how to manage all the relationships in your life and set strict priorities with marriage near the top and schedule time every day to minister to the needs of your spouse.

- **Past Baggage** – Work through your wounds, programming, and past mistakes; help your spouse process his or her pain, programming, and past.

I have rescued a number of marriages that were heading for divorce by using this simple chart. People have a choice to avoid disaster if given the understanding they need. If we know why there's a problem, we can determine how to fix it, but if every conversation grows more complicated because we don't listen to each other, it seems easier to give up in frustration.

Ignoring Needs	Immature Behaviors	Clashing Temperaments	Competing Relationships	Past Baggage

Let me remind you again of the premise of this book and its crucial details. Marital Intelligence means understanding the five problems in marriage and their solutions. If your marriage is not doing well, the problem is in one or more of those areas. If your marriage is okay but could be better, one of these five is what is preventing growth. If you have a good marriage but want it launched into the category of great marriages, one of these five is the answer. *There are only five problems in marriage.* Let me again review the five problems with you in a little bit more depth.

The first problem in marriage is the problem of needs. A marriage can become a business relationship with functionality but little pizzazz. When a marriage goes cold, it is because the love flow between the two has ceased. Love is not a mystery; it is simply meeting needs, pursuing, and pleasing. When both partners practice these three actions, the spark returns to a marriage quickly. One marriage counselor suggests couples return to what made them fall in love in the first place. Men and women need different things relationally out of their marriage. We crave the focused attention of one person who will selflessly fill our needs in these areas. When we find that special someone who will commit to meeting our needs, he or she is like a cool drink in the desert. If this someone fills up all our relational needs, we are drawn to marry that person and have him or her in our life forever.

The second problem in marriage is the problem of SAD behaviors. These three letters stand for selfish, angry, and destructive behaviors. These behaviors have at least three different levels of expressions. First, we all do selfish, angry, and destructive things from time to time. We didn't mean to cause damage to our marriage, but it happened. If that is the case, apologize and find a way to prevent it from happening again.

Second, we often do the opposite of what our spouse needs us to do, and we wound them doubly. It is those anti-need thrusts that wound so very deeply. They include sarcasm, yelling, staying at work longer, the silent treatment, hitting a wall, pornography, emotional distance, and walking away, among others. When we wound in those ways, apologies, alignment of expectations, and clarifying conversations are needed.

Finally, some marriage partners will be involved in poor behaviors so damaging that one incident could destroy the marriage. They include affairs, domestic violence, gambling away the house, addiction to drugs or alcohol, pornography, and prostitution, among others. In those cases significant change is needed with the help of a counselor and a proven battle plan. Marriages do not improve when both partners become equally selfish. They improve when love, patience, and clarity are introduced into the marriage.

If you find yourself caught in a cycle of stupidity and selfishness, think through what you've contributed to the mess and admit your guilt. Let the other person tell you how much he or she was hurt by what you did or did not do. Admit you were wrong. Ask for forgiveness. Assure your partner that you will not do the same thing again. Test to see if your honest apology was accepted and then move forward.

The third problem facing marriages is temperament. Opposites attract until they are married. Then it doesn't take long before differences in the way we live and think become apparent. What the other person thinks about and does is so different, it seems wrong. Realize the other person has internal impulses different from yours. The other person has a completely different background and was wired differently. Viva la difference! Enjoy the difference! The goal is not to have your way proved right all the time. The goal is to have an enjoyable relationship with your mate. Too many people keep score of how many times each one is right and how many each is wrong. No one needs to keep score. You both win when you have a vibrant relationship. Rejoice that God has given you a partner who comes at life differently. That will allow you to make fewer mistakes and bring great energy and perspectives to the situation. Learn to understand and accept your spouse for the way he or she thinks, for his or her internal drives, and the way your partner prefers to live.

The fourth problem facing marriage is competing relationships. We get so busy that we often let our marriages slip to the back burner of our lives. If we are not careful, the other relationships in our life will take all our time, energy, and money. Every day our marriages need attention. Every day our marriages can improve through focused attention. Many times the problems of life scream so loudly there is no time to invest in our marriages. There are times when an emergency puts other aspects of our life on hold, but we must eventually return to balanced living. Lurching from crisis to crisis is not healthy. We must establish a biblical priority structure for giving our time to the various relationships in our life. Only in that way can we get off the rat race treadmill. There are people who constantly live in crisis mode where only the loud "needy" relationship gets any attention. That is a disastrous way to live. We must allocate our time, energy, and resources according to the priorities of our relationships, not according to the crisis.

We have ten major relationships in our lives. We must understand how to bring order to each relationship and then put them in proper prioritized order. To lead a full life, we need to have all ten relationships functioning in some state of normalcy.

God	
Self	
Marriage	
Family	
Work	
Church	
Money	
Society	
Friends	
Enemies	

Every one of the ten major relationships is screaming for more time, energy, money, and effort, but we have only 168 hours a week. We must learn to assign the appropriate time to each of the relationships. When an area takes up too much out of our week, one of the other relationships suffers. One or more of your relationships will get less time than it needs; don't let it be your marriage. The wound of a failed marriage is much deeper than you can imagine.

The fifth problem that marriages face is the problem of past baggage. We carry with us pain, programming, and mistakes from our history. Those are affecting us here and now. There are times when the impact of past baggage issues is so strong that it must be dealt with before real progress can be attempted. We must act to understand how we've been damaged by past relationships, actions, and programming. Once we comprehend it, we can assign the proper amount of blame, seek justice, and forgive.

We have default ways we respond and react to certain situations. It's easy to overlook the impact of these hidden ways of acting and speaking, so we must examine and evaluate them as to whether they are effective. Learning a new way of acting, responding, and speaking is difficult but well worth it. God has a better operating program—one that produces harmony and vibrancy in relationships instead of fighting, tension, and distance.

There are many marriages that will never be right until underlying issues from the past are dealt with successfully. Do not permit what you are avoiding to destroy the relationships you so desperately need. Don't let your own issues keep you from ministering effectively to your spouse.

Marriage is not overly complicated. There are five main problems that can derail any marriage, but these problems have solutions. Even if only one spouse is willing to work on them at first, it is often enough to put the marriage on the right track to health and quality. Don't give up on your marriage. When you gain marital intelligence, the problems can be solved.

Appendices

Appendix #1
Marital Intelligence Test

This test probes the actions necessary to have a great marriage. Do not be surprised by the results. Celebrate your strengths and work on improving your weaknesses. Your spouse might respond differently to the same questions. These areas of differences are opportunities to grow and improve your marriage. Hopefully, this test will whet your appetite for the solutions in this book.

(Test begins on following page)

Marital Intelligence Test

Respond to the following statements using the following scale:
0 = Never; 1 = Rarely; 2 = Occasionally; 3 = Sometimes; 4 = Usually; 5 = Always

Problem #1: Needs

I compliment my spouse every day.	0 1 2 3 4 5
I understand and accept how my spouse thinks.	0 1 2 3 4 5
I am involved in our home and family to the satisfaction of my spouse.	0 1 2 3 4 5
My spouse feels secure financially, emotionally, physically, and morally.	0 1 2 3 4 5
I touch my spouse tenderly and hug him/her often.	0 1 2 3 4 5
I talk and listen to my spouse about an hour each day.	0 1 2 3 4 5
My spouse and I go on a date once a week.	0 1 2 3 4 5
I give my spouse at least one hour of focused attention each day.	0 1 2 3 4 5
I admire my spouse and he/she knows it.	0 1 2 3 4 5
I have adapted to my spouse's likes, dislikes, career, style, schedule, etc.	0 1 2 3 4 5
I work hard to make sure our home and family are the best they can be.	0 1 2 3 4 5
I meet my spouse's sexual needs.	0 1 2 3 4 5
I do things with my spouse that he/she enjoys.	0 1 2 3 4 5
I work hard at being grateful, kind, sympathetic, healthy, and attractive to my spouse.	0 1 2 3 4 5
I pursue the soul of my spouse by listening to what he/she says and doesn't say.	0 1 2 3 4 5

My spouse and I come to agreement before we make major decisions.	0 1 2 3 4 5
I receive a compliment daily from my spouse.	0 1 2 3 4 5
I believe my spouse understands the real me and does not demand that I change.	0 1 2 3 4 5
I feel that my spouse is fully engaged in the life of our family.	0 1 2 3 4 5
I am confident that my spouse would never damage our relationship financially, emotionally, verbally, physically, sexually, or morally.	0 1 2 3 4 5
I receive enough hugs and nonsexual touches from my spouse to meet my emotional needs.	0 1 2 3 4 5
My spouse actively listens to me daily.	0 1 2 3 4 5
I feel that my spouse wants to be with me romantically, mentally, and physically.	0 1 2 3 4 5
I feel admired and respected by my spouse.	0 1 2 3 4 5
My likes, dislikes, ideas, and desires are reflected in our relationship.	0 1 2 3 4 5
I enjoy spending time at home with my family.	0 1 2 3 4 5
My spouse understands and meets my sexual needs.	0 1 2 3 4 5
My spouse enjoys doing things together that are important to me.	0 1 2 3 4 5
I am more attracted to my spouse each year because he/she is kinder, more grateful, more encouraging, and takes care of him/herself.	0 1 2 3 4 5
I feel my spouse cares deeply for the real me.	0 1 2 3 4 5
Subtotal Section #1	

Problem #2: Behaviors

0 = Never; 1 = Rarely; 2 = Occasionally; 3 = Sometimes; 4 = Usually; 5 = Always

I avoid doing things I know annoy or damage my spouse.	0 1 2 3 4 5
I have calm, thoughtful conversations with my spouse about areas of concern rather than forcing him or her to guess.	0 1 2 3 4 5
I eliminate selfish or destructive behaviors that could be harmful.	0 1 2 3 4 5
I admit when I am wrong and apologize effectively.	0 1 2 3 4 5
I am open to correction and direction about actions, activities, and people that damage our marriage.	0 1 2 3 4 5
I listen when my spouse is pointing out something I have done wrong.	0 1 2 3 4 5
I am willing to grow and change to improve my marriage.	0 1 2 3 4 5
I realize that my marriage will have trouble, and I will need to apologize.	0 1 2 3 4 5
I try to understand my spouse's point of view rather than increase my intensity to get my way.	0 1 2 3 4 5
I align my expectations with my spouse ahead of time about schedules, plans, and actions.	0 1 2 3 4 5
When I feel angry with my spouse, I try to love him/her more effectively by meeting his/her needs rather than scolding, correcting, or distancing myself.	0 1 2 3 4 5
I make changes that my spouse thinks will help our marriage.	0 1 2 3 4 5
I have had hard conversations with my spouse about improvements needed in our marriage.	0 1 2 3 4 5

I am patient with my spouse's areas of weakness, allowing God time to make changes.	0 1 2 3 4 5
My spouse avoids things that annoy or irritate me.	0 1 2 3 4 5
My spouse tells me directly when he/she is angry with me rather than in another indirect way.	0 1 2 3 4 5
My spouse eliminates destructive behaviors that could destroy our marriage.	0 1 2 3 4 5
My spouse admits when he/she is wrong and truly apologizes.	0 1 2 3 4 5
My spouse is gracious, adaptable, and defers whenever possible.	0 1 2 3 4 5
My spouse listens and makes changes when I point out something he/she has done wrong.	0 1 2 3 4 5
My spouse is willing to grow and change to make our marriage better.	0 1 2 3 4 5
My spouse does not expect our marriage to be perfect and is willing to admit he/she is wrong.	0 1 2 3 4 5
My spouse tries to understand my point of view rather than walking away or becoming angry.	0 1 2 3 4 5
My spouse has had hard conversations with me about how he/she really feels about our marriage.	0 1 2 3 4 5
My spouse works hard at loving me even when I am hard to love.	0 1 2 3 4 5
My spouse initiates the alignment of our expectations about schedules, plans, and potential actions.	0 1 2 3 4 5
Subtotal Section #2	

Problem #3: Temperament

0 = Never; 1 = Rarely; 2 = Occasionally; 3 = Sometimes; 4 = Usually; 5 = Always

I accept my spouse the way he/she is without trying to change him/her.	0 1 2 3 4 5
I understand how my spouse's gender makes him/her different.	0 1 2 3 4 5
I know my spouse's dominant love languages.	0 1 2 3 4 5
I know how to speak my spouse's dominant love language.	0 1 2 3 4 5
I know whether my spouse is an extrovert or an introvert and how to value that and allow for it.	0 1 2 3 4 5
I know whether my spouse is an abstract thinker or a concrete thinker and how to value that and allow for it.	0 1 2 3 4 5
I realize how my spouse prefers to make decisions either objectively or personally and make allowances for that preference whenever possible.	0 1 2 3 4 5
I make room for my spouse's need for closure or spontaneity.	0 1 2 3 4 5
I understand my spouse's inner impulse for attention, control, peace, or perfection and do not demand that he/she change.	0 1 2 3 4 5
I feel accepted, not belittled or ignored by my spouse.	0 1 2 3 4 5
My unique point of view as a man or woman is valued and encouraged by my spouse.	0 1 2 3 4 5
My spouse knows my dominant love languages.	0 1 2 3 4 5
My spouse speaks love to me in my love language.	0 1 2 3 4 5

My spouse respects my extroversion or introversion and does not demand that I be something I'm not.	0 1 2 3 4 5
My spouse allows me to use my thinking style (abstract or concrete) without demanding that I be different.	0 1 2 3 4 5
My spouse and I understand and use my preference for objective or personal decisions to enhance our decisions and marriage.	0 1 2 3 4 5
If possible, my spouse allows me to bring closure to a situation or delay decisions, so I am comfortable.	0 1 2 3 4 5
My spouse knows my strongest internal impulse (attention, control, peace, or perfection) and, whenever possible, lets me be me.	0 1 2 3 4 5
Subtotal Section #3	

Problem #4: Relationships

0 = Never; 1 = Rarely; 2 = Occasionally; 3 = Sometimes; 4 = Usually; 5 = Always

I encourage my spouse to have a strong relationship with God.	0 1 2 3 4 5
I help my spouse take time for himself/herself.	0 1 2 3 4 5
I take time for myself to be refreshed and rested.	0 1 2 3 4 5
I demonstrate that my spouse and our marriage are more important than our children.	0 1 2 3 4 5
I place my marriage and children ahead of my extended family.	0 1 2 3 4 5
I take time daily to get away from work and focus on my wife, family, and home life.	0 1 2 3 4 5
I make sure that we have vacations and family times.	0 1 2 3 4 5
I demonstrate that my marriage is more important than our church or charity involvements.	0 1 2 3 4 5
I am responsible in earning, managing, and giving our money.	0 1 2 3 4 5
I demonstrate that my marriage is more important than my community and/or civic involvements.	0 1 2 3 4 5
I put appropriate amounts of time into all the major arenas of my life.	0 1 2 3 4 5
I demonstrate that my marriage is more important than my friends.	0 1 2 3 4 5
I demonstrate that my marriage is more important than my competitors, enemies, bosses, and/or oppressors.	0 1 2 3 4 5
My spouse encourages me to have a strong relationship with God.	0 1 2 3 4 5

My spouse encourages me to be healthy spiritually, mentally, emotionally, and physically and to take time for myself.	0 1 2 3 4 5
My spouse demonstrates that our marriage is more important than our children.	0 1 2 3 4 5
My spouse puts our marriage and our children ahead of his/her extended family.	0 1 2 3 4 5
My spouse makes sure every day that he/she disengages from work and focuses for some period of time on our marriage, home, and family.	0 1 2 3 4 5
My spouse makes sure that we have vacations and family times.	0 1 2 3 4 5
My spouse demonstrates our marriage is more important than his/her church or charitable involvements.	0 1 2 3 4 5
My spouse is responsible in gaining, managing, and giving our money.	0 1 2 3 4 5
My spouse demonstrates that our marriage is more important than his/her community or civic involvements.	0 1 2 3 4 5
My spouse demonstrates that our marriage is more important than his/her friends.	0 1 2 3 4 5
My spouse demonstrates that our marriage is more important than his/her competitors, enemies, bosses, and/or oppressors.	0 1 2 3 4 5
My spouse puts an appropriate amount of time in all the major arenas of his/her life.	0 1 2 3 4 5
Subtotal Section #4	

Problem #5: Baggage

0 = Never; 1 = Rarely; 2 = Occasionally; 3 = Sometimes; 4 = Usually; 5 = Always

I am processing the pain of my past so that it does not damage my marriage.	0 1 2 3 4 5
I am aware and open about the deeply painful things in my life and how they impact my relationships.	0 1 2 3 4 5
I am supportive (financially, emotionally, and relationally) of my spouse's receiving the help he/she needs to overcome the issues and difficulties of his/her past.	0 1 2 3 4 5
I have changed behaviors I learned from my family that were damaging my relationships.	0 1 2 3 4 5
I am open to discussions about unhelpful and/or destructive patterns I have learned from my family.	0 1 2 3 4 5
I am open to discussions about unhelpful and/or destructive patterns I have learned from my culture or heritage.	0 1 2 3 4 5
I have done all I can to bring healing to the destructive behavior in my past so it does not damage my present relationships.	0 1 2 3 4 5
My spouse is aware of and open about the traumatic events of his or her past that impact his or her relationships.	0 1 2 3 4 5
My spouse is processing the pain of his or her past so that it will not damage our marriage.	0 1 2 3 4 5
My spouse is supportive of my receiving the help I need to deal with the issues of my past.	0 1 2 3 4 5
My spouse is open to discussions and change in areas of unhelpful and/or destructive patterns he/she learned from his/her family.	0 1 2 3 4 5
My spouse is open to discussions and change in areas of unhelpful and/or destructive patterns he/she learned from his/her culture or heritage.	0 1 2 3 4 5

My spouse admits foolish, selfish, and/or destructive behaviors of the past and has done all he or she can so that they have the least impact in the present.	0 1 2 3 4 5
Subtotal Section #5	
Subtotal Section #4	
Subtotal Section #3	
Subtotal Section #2	
Subtotal Section #1	
Total of all Sections	

Appendix #2

Marital Intelligence Test Results and Scoring

Under 100

At this point your marriage is staying together because of the commitment you made. There is little drawing you and your spouse to each other. While there may be lots of hurt already, your marriage can improve through specific actions designed to meet the deepest relational needs of your spouse. Don't wait for improvement before acting; start loving your partner first.

101-200

This is a neutral marriage. It is not really negative and not really positive. Staying together is still largely a commitment instead of "I could never leave my best friend!" Unfortunately, many of these kinds of marriages break up when the kids leave or if someone better comes along. Just a few of the actions mentioned in this test would make a big difference in your marriage.

201-300

This is a good marriage—better than most. There is love and hope for something even better. Both of you are trying to be content with the few needs that are being met. You may say, "This is as good as it gets. Who are we to want more?" But whole sections of relational needs are not being met. This provides temptation a place to strike and pull your marriage apart. Often this marriage begins to die because of boredom and lack of proper focus. The relationship grows boring for lack of energy put into it—particularly in the area of meeting needs.

301-400

You have what most people call a great marriage. You are two people who love one another and are working for a common purpose. There are not a lot of fights or disagreements. There is, however, more that could be gained by increasing the level of love in your marriage. Relational needs are met intermittently rather than consistently. One person is probably supplying a more significant amount of energy than the other. It's good one person believes in and supports the marriage, but it is time for both parties to join this marriage with full engagement.

401- 500

This is an irresistible marriage in which both parties are consistently drawn to each other. You meet each other's needs, which makes the other person irresistible. Being married is pure joy as you mutually meet your partner's needs. It is a delight to be married when you love each other like this. There is always room for improvement and even more love in your marriage. There is always 500+! Keep enjoying each other!

Appendix #3

Recreational Companionship Ideas

Circle the activities that you enjoy or would be willing to try. This list is taken from *Becoming a Godly Wife* by Gil and Dana Stieglitz. If spending two to six hours a week focused on something could significantly improve your marriage, would you do it? Marriages stay together because two people find pleasure in each other's company.

Building Things	Watching TV	Learning
Crafts	Movies	Flying
Racing	Eating	Bike Riding
Working on Cars	Sleeping	Jogging
Sewing	Tennis	Amusement Parks
Crochet	Racquetball	Roller Coasters
Cricket	Golf	Pets
Volleyball	Talking	Pinball
Football	Waterskiing	Air Hockey
Basketball	Boating	Table Games
Spear fishing	Traveling	Playing Music
Swimming	Photography	Listening to Music
Snow Skiing	Developing Pictures	Opera
Cross Country Skiing	Watching Football	Concerts
Tubing, Tobogganing	Watching Baseball	Singing
Snowmobiling	Hiking	Parties
Motorcycles	Working Out	Baking
ATV	Karate	Drawing
4 Wheeling	Judo	Modeling
Reading	Improvisational Games	Snorkeling

Scuba Diving	RV Shows	Kayaking
Rollerblading	Bowling	Historic Sites
Roller Hockey	Hang Gliding	Conventions
Ice Hockey	Sky Diving	Retreats
Ice Skating	Museum	Speaking
Camping	Professional Sports	Backpacking
Competitive Running	Spelunking	Triathlon
Softball	Mountain Climbing	Marathon running
Water parks	Gardening	Soccer
Horseshoes	Woodworking	Quilting
Beach Volleyball	Bird Watching	Embroidery
Darts	Shopping	Bow Hunting
Frisbee Golf	Used Booking	Rifle Hunting
Archery	Wind Surfing	Investing
Flying	Table Tennis	Calligraphy
Ultralights	Cooking	Video Games
Sailing	Writing	Arcades
Motor Boating	Acting	Shuffleboard
Nature Walks	Community Projects	Hiking
Flying RC Airplanes	Disabled Ministries	Making Money
Beach	Special Needs	Taking Classes
Beach Games	Books on Tape	New business
Horseback Riding	Driving	Seminars
Going Out to Eat	Painting	Debating
Fishing	Auto Repair/Detailing	Church
Aerobics	White Water Rafting	Ministry
Pottery	Picnic Games	Bed & Breakfasts
Antiquing	Laser Tag	Charitable work
Boat Shows	Rock Climbing	Walking
Home & Garden Shows	Canoeing	Sightseeing Tours

End Notes

End Notes

Notes for the Introduction

[1] Harley, *Fall in love, Stay in love*, 11

[2] I began doing this "new" type of marriage counseling in the mid 1980s, and I was pleased to see others doing it also as I read various books in the 1990s. In reality it is a counseling based upon the biblical directives of ministering to one's spouse. It takes seriously the directives to meet your spouse's needs and love him or her first (Matthew 7:12) before they do it for you.

Notes for Problem # 1: Ignoring Needs

[1] For years I have been helping marriages by detailing the scriptural commands for men and women. (See Ephesians 5:22-31; 1 Peter 3:1-8; Colossians 3:18, 19; Genesis 2:24; 1 Corinthians 7:1-5; Song of Solomon; Proverbs 5; 7; 8; 9; 14:12; 18:24.) It is in these ways that both husbands and wives demonstrate love in their marriage. After becoming very familiar with these commands and needs, I began to notice how a husband's needs and a wife's needs were different sides of the same coin. I recognized seven basic relational needs that are essential for a great marriage. They are Value, Acceptance, Leadership, Attraction, Friendship, Intimacy and Pursuit. The more these relational needs flow between husband and wife, the stronger the marriage. The less these relational needs are met, the weaker the marriage.

[2] In *Becoming a Godly Husband* and *Becoming a Godly Wife* my wife and I discuss in a much more complete way how to meet the deepest relational needs of men and women.

[3] At times there are exceptions to gender generalizations. Some needs may be reversed, such as the husband may need understanding and the wife respect. I have found such exceptions in fewer than 30 percent of my cases, however, but it does occur.

[4] Sax, *Why Gender Matters*, 83

[5] Ibid., 19

[6] Harley, *His Needs, Her Needs,* 147

[7] Sax, 29

[8] Ibid., 29

[9] Ibid., 29

Notes for Problem #2: Immature Behaviors

[1] Powell, *Why Am I Afraid to Tell You Who I Am?,* 105-153

Notes for Problem #3: Clashing Temperaments

[1] Sax, 4

[2] Ibid., 18

[3] Ibid., 22

[4] Ibid., 19

[5] Ibid., 29

[6] Ibid., 25, 26

[7] Ibid,, 37

[8] Ibid., 37

[9] Stieglitz, *Mission Possible*, 191

[10] Sax, 59

[11] Ibid., 107

[12] Ibid., 69

[13] Ibid., 69

[14] Ibid., 61

[15] Ibid., 62

[16] Ibid., 83

[17] Ibid., 83

[18] Ibid., 83

[19] Tieger and Barron-Tieger, *Do What You Are*

[20] Ibid., 20

[21] Ibid., 21

[22] Ibid., 21
[23] Ibid., 23
[24] Ibid., 26
[25] Ibid., 26
[26] Ibid., 26
[27] Littauer, *Personality Plus*
[28] Chapman, *The Five Love Languages*
[29] Ibid., 15
[30] Ibid., 97
[31] Ibid., 115
[32] Ibid., 81
[33] Ibid., 59
[34] Ibid., 39

Notes for Problem #4: Competing Relationships

[1] Dave Ramsey, Financial Peace University. (www.daveramsey.com).
[2] Larry Burkett, Crown Financial Ministries. (www.crown.org).
[3] Ron Blue, Mastering Your Money. (www.mastermoney.org; www.ronblue.com).
[4] Willow Creek Association. Good Sense. (www.goodsenseministry.org).
[5] Sherbondy, *Changing Your Child's Heart*
[6] Barna, Leading Your Church Forward Conference handouts, 35

If parents are willing to be involved in 10 of the following 12 "Active Parenting" processes, they will virtually eliminate substance abuse (alcohol, tobacco, drugs) from their children's lives:

1. Monitoring TV use
2. Monitoring Internet use
3. Restricting CDs purchased/listened to
4. Knowing the child's whereabouts at all times
5. Being told the truth about the activity: who, what, where, when, etc.
6. Awareness of academic performance
7. Imposing and enforcing a curfew
8. Adult home when child returns from school
9. Eat dinner together six - seven times per week
10. TV is turned off during dinner

11. Children are assigned and accountable for chores
12. There is predetermined, known response to substance abuse: extremely upset

Notes for Problem #5: Past Baggage

[1] Scazzero, *Emotionally Healthy Spirituality*
[2] Scazzero, *The Emotionally Healthy Church*

Bibliography

Bibliography

Barna, George. Notes from the Leading Your Church Forward Conference, First Baptist Church of Elk Grove, November 2003.

Blue, Ron. "Mastering Your Money." Video or DVD series. (www.mastermoney.org; www.ronblue.com).

Burkett, Larry. Crown Financial Ministries. (www.crown.org).

Chapman, Gary. *The Five Love Languages*. (Chicago: Northfield Publishing), 1995.

Harley, Willard F. *Fall in Love, Stay in Love*. (Grand Rapids: Fleming H. Revell), 2001.

_____. *His Needs, Her Needs: Building an Affair-Proof Marriage*. (Grand Rapids: Fleming H. Revell), 2001.

Littauer, Florence. *Personality Plus*. (Grand Rapids: Fleming H. Revell), 1992.

Ramsey, Dave. Financial Peace University. (www.daveramsey.com).

Sax, Leonard. *Why Gender Matters*. (New York: Random House), 2005.

Scazzero, Pete. *Emotionally Healthy Spirituality*. (Franklin, Tenn.: Integrity Publishing), 2006 .

_____. *The Emotionally Healthy Church*. (Grand Rapids: Zondervan), 2003.

Sherbondy, Steve. *Changing Your Child's Heart*. (Wheaton, Ill.: Tyndale House Publishing), 1998.

Stieglitz, Gil. *Becoming a Godly Husband*. (Enumclaw, Wash.: Wine Press Publications), 2001.

_____. *Mission Possible: Winning the Battle Over Temptation*. (Cleveland, Tenn.: Pathway Press), 2006.

Stieglitz, Gil and Dana Stieglitz. *Becoming a Godly Wife*. (Cleveland, Tenn.: Pathway Press), 2005.

Tieger, Paul D. and Barbara Barron-Tieger. *Do What You Are*. (Boston, Mass.: Little, Brown and Company), 1992.

Willow Creek Association. Good Sense. (www.goodsenseministry.org).

Other Resources by
Gil Stieglitz
www.ptlb.com

BOOKS
Spiritual Disciplines of a C.H.R.I.S.T.I.A.N.
Becoming a Godly Husband
Becoming a Godly Wife, Co-authored with Dana Stieglitz
Biblical Meditation: The Key to Biblical Life Transformation
Mission Possible: Winning the Battle Over Temptation
Breaking Satanic Bondage
Keeping Visitors
Snapshots in the Life of Jesus

VIDEOS
"Growing a Vibrant and Healthy Church"
"Marital Intelligence: There Are Only Five Problems in Marriage"
"Spiritual Disciplines of a C.H.R.I.S.T.I.A.N" *(Master's Level Series)*

AUDIO
"The Ten Commandments"
"God's Principles for Handling Money"
"Four Essentials of Great Parenting"
"Becoming a Godly Parent"

If you would like to schedule Dr. Gil Stieglitz
to speak to your group, contact him at *www.ptlb.com*.